ROSES

ROSES

INSPIRATIONS FOR BEAUTIFUL GIFTS, CRAFTS AND DISPLAYS

GILLY LOVE

PHOTOGRAPHS BY MICHELLE GARRETT

LORENZ BOOKS

NEW YORK • LONDON • SYDNEY • BATH

For Rob, who has given me my first garden to grow roses with passion

This edition published in 1996 by Lorenz Books
an imprint of Anness Publishing Limited
administrative office: 27 West 20th Street
New York, NY 10011.

© 1996 Anness Publishing Limited

Lorenz Books are available for bulk purchase for sales promotion and for premium use. For details write or call the manager of special sales, LORENZ BOOKS, 27 West 20th Street, New York, NY 10011; (212) 807-6739.

Produced by Anness Publishing Limited
1 Boundary Row
London SE1 8HP

ISBN 1 85967 211 6

Publisher: JOANNA LORENZ
Editorial Manager: HELEN SUDELL
Designer: LISA TAI
Photographer: MICHELLE GARRETT

Printed and bound in Hong Kong

CONTENTS

Introduction

Oh, no man knows through what
wild centuries roves back the rose.

WALTER DE LA MARE (1873–1956)

ℐNTRODUCTION

There can be few greater sensual pleasures than walking through a garden of exquisitely scented roses or receiving a bouquet of freshly picked full blooms whose heady perfume fills an entire room. Roses have inspired poets and philosophers, kings and queens since the earliest civilizations and continue to be the passion of gardeners all over the world. This book traces the history of this remarkable species; details the myths and legends surrounding it and illustrates why the rose is the world's most loved and most prized flower. The ancestors of these plants are now, hundreds of years later, being used to provide new varieties that have all the distinct old rose qualities of voluptuous shape and alluring perfume but that can flower virtually constantly, from early summer until the first frosts.

Roses are now being planted with other aromatic plants in beautiful color-coordinated borders, and traditional rose arbours and arches are enjoying a happy revival. Even the smallest terrace or balcony can benefit from scented roses scrambling up roofs and walls entwined with honeysuckles and perfumed clematis. Miniature and the newer patio roses are ideal for tiny gardens, content to grow in tubs and pots along with lavenders and other aromatic herbs.

Rose essential oil featured in nearly half of all medicinal remedies until the nineteenth century, and the ancient art of aromatherapy, which combines essential oils with massage, uses this precious oil to treat depression, menstrual disorders and as a general tonic for the nervous, circulatory and respiratory systems.

Throughout this book there are inspirational ideas for decorating your home with roses, both fresh and dried, making delightful presents for family and friends, effective beauty formulas for face and body and easy-to-follow recipes for delicious sweets, traditional desserts and some authentic Balti dishes.

Roses are unique for providing stimulation and nourishment for all of the senses, and no garden is complete without them. The world's oldest living rose is said to be the Rose of Hildesham, a form of *Rosa canina* or the dog rose, which was planted by the walls of Hildesham cathedral in Germany on the orders of Emperor Charlemagne around 815 AD. It has survived several serious fires, withstood serious diseases and was almost destroyed during the Second World War, but it continues to flower every year as a testament to this magnificent plant's ability to endure and flourish and to give inspiration to rose lovers the world over.

ROSES - THEIR HISTORY

Prized, cherished and fought over for centuries, roses now grow all over the world, although they are almost certainly indigenous to the northern hemisphere. Rose fossils, millions of years old, have been found only north of the equator, suggesting that those species now growing in South Africa, Australia and New Zealand were taken there by emigrants eager to establish a familiar plant from their native countries.

The wild rose was most certainly enjoyed by early people for its sweet petals and tasty hips, and rose cultivation probably began around five thousand years ago in China and in what is now Iraq, where references to roses have been found in ancient tombs at Ur. In the *Iliad*, Homer's epic on the siege of Troy composed around 1200 BC, the poet tells of Achilles's shield being decorated with roses to celebrate his victory over Hector. Hector's body was also anointed with rose oil before it was embalmed. The roses mentioned by many Greek historians were almost certainly *Rosa gallica*, the ancestor of numerous European roses. Known as the 'Apothecary's Rose' or 'Red Damask,' *R. g. officinalis* was the main source of rose oil and medicinal remedies in Europe before the introduction of rose species from the Far East.

A page from an illuminated manuscript showing the arms of Henry VII. It is decorated on all four sides by what came to be known as the Tudor Rose.

The early Christian church condemned roses as a symbol of depravity, with some justification, since Nero's obsession with these flowers almost certainly contributed to the fall of the Roman Empire. The emperor's excesses were notorious and it is said that tons of roses were required for the numerous banquets he gave where guests sat on pillows stuffed with them. Vast quantities of petals were showered over people at orgies, reputedly suffocating one participant, and pure rose water baths were offered to all guests. Roses symbolized success to the Romans and thousands of petals would be threaded onto brass wires to make garlands and headdresses. Peasants and farmers therefore came to believe that it was more profitable to grow roses than corn, a disastrous misconception noted by the Roman poet Horace and other intellectuals of his time.

Little information exists about the cultivation of roses following the collapse of the Roman Empire until about 400 AD when the church adopted the white *R. alba* as the emblem of the Virgin Mary. In 1272, Edward I of England, upon his return from the last Crusade, ordered rose trees to be planted in the gardens of the Tower of London and chose a gold rose as his own symbol. It is possible that returning Crusaders were responsible for the introduction of *R. damascena*, the damask rose. Certainly by the end of the fifteenth century the rose 'Autumn Damask', known in France as 'Quatre Saisons' and the first rose in Europe to produce two crops of flowers every summer, was growing in English gardens.

It is debatable whether *R. gallica* was brought to England by the Romans or at a later date by returning Crusaders. It was, however, the emblem of the house of Lancaster in their prolonged struggle against the house of York (who adopted *R. alba*) during the bitter Wars of the Roses in England in the fifteenth century. The marriage of Henry Tudor (Henry VII) and Elizabeth of York finally united the factions. Their emblem was a white rose in the center of a red rose entwined with a crown. Since then the British royal family have adopted the rose as their own: the tragic Mary Queen of Scots so loved roses that she worked them into many of her legendary embroideries. By the end of the sixteenth century, *R. foetida* had been introduced into Europe from what was then Persia and *R. moschata*, the 'Musk Rose', was certainly favored by the court of Henry VIII.

Roses were taken to America by the Pilgrim Fathers and by the beginning of the seventeenth century were growing in many gardens in Massachusetts. North America has its own wild roses, *R. virginiana* and *R. carolina*, and although these roses have not contributed to the development of hybrids, another variety, *R. setigera*, has produced some vigorous ramblers including 'Baltimore Belle', still famous in America, and 'Long John Silver', a fragrant pure white rose which is a favorite of Peter Beales, one of Britain's most respected rose-growers and experts.

The excesses of Roman life are clearly shown in this banqueting scene, with garlands of roses adorning some of the guests' heads.

From this period, Dutch rose breeders developed the *R. centifolia*, also known as the Provence or cabbage rose because of its "hundred-petalled flowers." Moss roses appeared around the mid-eighteenth century as a sport from a *centifolia*, that is to say a mutation or a seedling markedly different from its parent. Roses apparently lost some of their popularity in the seventeenth and early eighteenth centuries but enjoyed a revival of interest when the Empress Josephine, first wife of Napoleon, sent servants all over the world to discover new roses for her garden at Malmaison near Paris, where she eventually

Empress Josephine, the beautiful first wife of Napoleon Bonaparte, seen here in her apartments at Malmaison. Even during the Napoleonic Wars, Josephine was said to have corresponded with English rose growers to obtain new species for her garden.

grew more than 250 varieties. Thanks to her patronage of the artist Pierre-Joseph Redouté, exquisite paintings record many of the specimens planted in the garden.

The Chinese had been growing roses for thousands of years, and around 1781 a pink rose, *R. chinensis*, now known as 'Old Blush', was planted in the Netherlands and soon came to England. Some years later a captain of the British East India Company returned home with a red form of the same rose that he had found growing in Calcutta, and it was named *R. semperflorens*, or the 'Bengal Rose' or 'Slater's Crimson China'. Between them these

two roses are responsible for the remontant or repeat-flowering qualities that are found in most modern roses.

Somewhat later, the flowers known as Tea roses, probably a cross between *R. gigantea* and *R. chinensis*, arrived via the ships of the British East India Company – their main cargo was tea, which probably accounts for the roses' common name. They became very fashionable in Europe and because many of them are quite tender, the Victorians grew them in grand conservatories along with other exotic flowers brought back by explorers and botanists from the vast British Empire.

One of the first marriages between a rose from the west and one from the east was a cross between 'Autumn Damask' and a red China rose, which was probably obtained from France by the 2nd Duchess of Portland, an enthusiastic rose gardener of the late eighteenth century. The Portland roses, as they became known, were very popular in the early 1800s and, though few have survived today, they are ideal for container growing, prized for their perfume and ability to flower throughout the summer.

Meanwhile, at around the same time in Charleston, South Carolina, a rice grower called John Champneys crossed a Musk rose, *R. moschata*, with a China rose, *R. chinensis* 'Parson's Pink China' or 'Old Blush', which had been a gift from his friend and neighbor Philippe Noisette. He gave the new seedlings

A botanical study of Rosa Carolina corymbosa, by the French artist Pierre-Joseph Redouté. His studies of roses are among the finest in the world.

between 'Old Blush' and 'Autumn Damask' found growing in rose hedges on the Ile de Bourbon in the Indian Ocean. Many of these Shrub roses are still available, including 'Louise Odier', 'Souvenir de la Malmaison' and the much prized, thornless 'Zéphirine Drouhin'.

Throughout Queen Victoria's reign, Hybrid Perpetuals were introduced as the result of complex breeding between Chinas, Portlands, Bourbons and Noisettes. Around the mid-eighteenth century a wild Rambler rose, *R. multiflora*, was introduced from Japan. It was to become the parent of the numerous Cluster-Flowered (Floribunda) modern roses. The birth of what is considered to be the first modern rose, the Large-Flowered shrub, more familiarly known as the Hybrid Tea, took place in 1867 with Jean-Baptiste Guillot's rose, patriotically named 'La France'. This new breed of roses satisfied the gardening requirements of neat, remontant shrubs with elegant and delicate flowers on plants that were truly winter-hardy.

Most rose-breeders of the twentieth century have concentrated their efforts on Large-Flowered shrubs and Cluster-Flowered shrubs in colors echoing current tastes in fashion. Since the late 1960s there has been a steady increase in the number of smaller shrubs for tiny gardens, patios and pots. At the same time, a new breed of rose, evocative of Dutch old masters and the romantic paintings of

Roses continued to be seen as a symbol of purity and innocence. Seen here is a painting of the Madonna of the Rosebush by Sandro Botticelli.

to Philippe who made more crosses and sent both seed and plants to his brother Louis in Paris. The first seedling he called 'Rosier de Philippe Noisette', a long name inevitably shortened to 'Noisette'. 'Blush Noisette' is still widely grown today and so too is the beautiful 'Madame Alfred Carrière', one of the few climbing roses that can tolerate a north-facing wall.

Bourbon roses also made their appearance about this period. These began as a cross

Pierre-Joseph Redouté, has been introduced by the English rose-grower, David Austin. He has raised roses that may be described as some of the finest reproductions, growing no more than 4 feet tall but with all the charm and scent of classic roses of the past, crossing Damasks and Gallicas with Modern Shrubs. Now owners of even the smallest garden may enjoy the delights of roses that the Empress Josephine would have considered for her garden at Malmaison.

ROSES ~ MYTHS AND FOLKLORE

For a flower that can trace its ancestry back for thousands of years, it is obviously difficult to separate fact from fiction and to differentiate between history and myth. Most cultures have fostered legends concerning roses and the Greek and Roman traditions are no exception. The rose, myrtle and apple were all sacred to Aphrodite – called Venus by the Romans – goddess of love.

At her birth, when she emerged from the sea standing on a giant scallop shell, rose petals are said to have rained from the sky. A Greek legend claims that when Aphrodite was rushing to her dying lover, Adonis, she scratched herself on a white rose hedge and red rose bushes grew up where drops of her blood fell. The Romans have a different legend, claiming that Jupiter was skulking around trying to catch a glimpse of Venus while she was bathing and the red rose was the result of her blushes. The rose's thorns are attributed to Cupid, the son of Venus, as one day he was stung by a bee and reacted by sending one of his arrows through a nearby rose bush, thus bestowing it with thorns for evermore.

The association of Venus and love with roses, myrtle and apples certainly continued until the nineteenth century, when every bride carried roses and at least a sprig of both myrtle

and apple blossom as good omens for her forthcoming marriage.

Another Greek legend has it that Rhodanthe, who was a queen of Corinth, sought refuge in the temple of Diana; this was granted, but her beauty was so great that the locals started to worship her in preference to the goddess. As a punishment for the insult to his sister, Apollo turned poor Rhodanthe into a rose bush.

Islamic tradition claims that roses were the

Bloody Queen Mary, wife of King Philip II of Spain, who became Queen Mary I of England, shown here holding the Tudor Rose.

tiny drops of sweat that formed when the prophet Mohammed perspired. But even within that culture there is not complete agreement, as another of its legends says the white rose was created because the lotus blossom closed its petals and slept at night. The red rose appeared because one night a nightingale fell in love with a white rose and during a very passionate embrace the bird's breast was pricked by a thorn and its blood turned the white roses red – or could this be the legend of how the robin got its red breast?

In the sixth century BC the Persian king Kyros II gave the rose regal status by adopting it as his emblem. One of the seven wonders of the ancient world – the hanging gardens of Babylon – was planted with roses by Nebuchadnezzar because they were his wife's favorite flower.

Little is known of the myths and legends from China, but the famous philosopher Confucius, who attended the imperial court in about 500 BC, wrote that there were at least six hundred books on roses. Hazel Le Rougetel, the writer and rose historian, visited China in 1982 and brought back a China tea rose whose original name is translated into English as "The Tipsy Imperial Concubine." This ancient rose, whose name must surely

originate in a legend, was introduced to the West by the leading rose grower Peter Beales.

During the sixteenth and seventeenth centuries, the London pewterers adopted the Tudor rose and a crown as a hallmark of fine quality and this may go some way to explaining why so many English pubs are called The Rose and Crown.

The classical myth of the Birth of Venus is beautifully portrayed here by Sandro Botticelli. As Venus arises from the sea, roses are strewn around her.

Roses have been popular with poets and playwrights throughout the centuries, and it was probably the Greek poetess Sappho who originally named the rose "The Queen of Flowers." The girl's name "Rose" implies beauty, valor and purity, as described in the "The Yellow Rose of Texas," the ballad written to honor Emily Morgan, an American heroine who helped the Texans win their freedom from the Mexicans. Some American states, including New York, Iowa and Georgia, have also adopted the rose as their state flower.

15

ROSES FOR HEALTH

Nicholas Culpeper, the English apothecary, physician and astrologer who practiced in the middle of the seventeenth century, praised the numerous virtues of roses in his book *The English Physician Enlarged* or *The Herbal*, proclaiming their healing properties for fevers, headaches, jaundice and joint aches as well as "fluxes and lasks of the belly." He noted the antiseptic and regenerative qualities of roses and made oils, vinegars, distilled waters and ointments from their petals, leaves and hips. He had most certainly studied the works of Dioscorides, a first-century physician who used the hips of *Rosa canina* (the dog rose), so called because its roots could allegedly cure rabies. It was also used to cure bladder disorders, for pain relief and as a general tonic.

Rosa omeiensis, which has delicate fernlike foliage, spectacular thorns and bright red hips.

Hundreds of years later the exceptionally high vitamin C content of rose hips proved invaluable when rose hip syrup was produced as a dietary supplement for children during the Second World War in both Britain and America. The high sugar content has made this syrup less popular today, but rose hips taken in tablet form or as an infusion are recommended as a natural source of vitamin C.

There are numerous roses that produce excellent hips including *R. rugosa* and its hybrids such as 'Frau Dagmar Hartopp', 'Hansa' and 'Scabrosa', and *R. moyesii*, in particular the hybrids 'Eddie's Jewel', 'Highdownensis' and 'Geranium'. People who are found to be suffering from anemia are often encouraged to increase their vitamin C intake in order to help them absorb any extra iron they are prescribed, either in food or as supplements, and drinking several cups of rose-hip tea every day is a pleasant and healthy way to achieve this.

Just as in ancient Rome, where women believed rose petals preserved beauty and youth, rose oil is still recommended by aromatherapists and naturopaths who advise combining a couple of drops of rose essential oil with jojoba, wheat-germ or almond oils, as a facial moisturizer for aging skin. An

Rose water may be used as a natural and very gentle facial toner for all skin types.

alternative treatment is to add a few drops of rose essential oil to a bowl of steaming water for a restorative and relaxing facial.

Many reputable natural cosmetic companies use essential rose oil in their formulas from moisturizers to hair conditioners and suggest rose water as a fragrant and soothing toner for all skin types.

Rose-hip Tea

Rose hips provide a sweet astringent tea which is high in vitamin C. As it is caffeine-free, this tea can be enjoyed all day either hot or iced – either plain or with a squeeze of lemon. Rose petals may also be made into a tea that is less astringent than rose-hip tea.

MAKES ABOUT 6 CUPS
$\frac{1}{3}$ cup rose hips
$6\frac{1}{4}$ cups filtered or bottled
still water

Trim the rose hips, then wash and dry them carefully. Soak the rose hips in a small bowl with enough water to cover them completely for about 24 hours. Bring the filtered or bottled water to boil in a nonreactive saucepan and add the rose hips. Simmer for about 30 minutes. Strain and serve, adding a little honey to sweeten if preferred. Alternatively, you can use dried rose petals by grinding enough to yield about ½ tsp.

Add boiling water, strain and serve.

Rose tea may be made from the hips or from dried petals. Shown above are 'Brown Velvet' roses.

Growing Roses

And I wove the thing to a random rhyme

For the Rose is Beauty, the gardener, Time.

AUSTIN DOBSON (1840–1921)

CHOOSING ROSES FOR YOUR GARDEN

Selecting roses to grow depends largely on personal taste, but it is also wise to consider the size of your garden, the other plants that are growing there and the role you want your roses to play. Rather than just choosing roses from a catalog, try to visit gardens in your area for ideas, and consult experts in local nurseries or some of the specialist rose growers whose recommendations are based on years of invaluable experience. Try to incorporate roses into an integral scheme in terms of shape and, of course, color.

Hedges of roses are a wonderful way to border a path or divide one part of the garden from another and some varieties can create such an impenetrable barrier that they make other forms of fencing unnecessary. Climbing roses not only decorate a wall but those with sharp thorns are both effective and attractive as a way of deterring burglars. Some roses have not only beautiful flowers but also exceptional hips in late summer and early autumn which provide an extra splash of color. For those with only a small patio or

Every autumn, Rosa macrophylla 'Arthur Hillier' produces flask-shaped drooping bright red hips.

For more than one hundred years the very fragrant lilac-pink Portland rose, 'Comte de Chambord' has made a perfect companion for blue and purple delphiniums.

sheltered balcony, it is still possible to grow some roses in containers though they will require extra watering and feeding in the growing season.

It is usually recommended that repeat flowering or remontant Shrub roses should be planted in groups of three of one variety in a triangle 18 inches apart so that they grow together to form one "shrub," which creates more impact in a border and makes their perfume more intense. Scent is the quality that attracts most gardeners to roses. Choose varieties with a strong fragrance to grow around an arch, up a wall or in a scentless part of the garden. With so many roses to choose from it seems inconceivable to me to select a rose without a perfume.

OLD GARDEN SHRUB ROSES WITH A PERFUME

'Belle de Crécy' (Gallica, gray pink); 'Celestial' (Alba, soft pink); 'Felicia' (Hybrid Musk, silvery salmon pink); 'Fimbriata' (*R. rugosa*, soft pink); 'Louise Odier' (Bourbon, bright pink); 'Madame Hardy' (Damask, white); 'Maiden's Blush' (Alba, soft pink); 'Parfum de l'Hay' (*R. rugosa*, deep red); 'Pax' (Hybrid Musk, cream-white); 'Quatre Saisons' (*R. damascena*, silver pink); 'Souvenir de la Malmaison' (Bourbon, pale pink).

MODERN GARDEN SHRUB ROSES WITH A PERFUME

'Alec's Red' (Large-Flowered, pink red); 'Anna Pavlova' (Shrub, pale pink); 'Blue Moon' (Large-Flowered, lilac mauve); 'The Dark Lady' (English, deep red); 'Elizabeth Harkness' (Large-Flowered, gray-pink); 'Gertrude Jekyll' (English, rich pink); 'Ingrid Bergman' (Large-Flowered, scarlet red); 'Just Joey' (Large-Flowered, copper); 'Sir Frederick Ashton' (Large-Flowered, white); 'Whisky Mac' (Large-Flowered, amber gold).

OLD CLIMBING ROSES WITH A PERFUME

'Gloire de Dijon' (climbing Tea, buff pink); 'Long John Silver' (*R. Setigera* hybrid climber, soft white); 'Madame Alfred Carrière' (climbing Noisette, blush white); 'Surpassing Beauty' (Hybrid Perpetual, deep crimson); 'Zéphirine Drouhin' (Bourbon, cerise pink).

MODERN CLIMBING ROSES WITH A PERFUME

'Alchemist' (deep yellow); 'Compassion' (pale copper); 'High Hopes' (cream pink); 'Malaga' (deep pink); 'Schoolgirl' (copper pink).

ROSES FOR TALL HEDGES

'Buff Beauty' (Hybrid Musk, pale apricot); 'Felicia' (Hybrid Musk, silver pink).

ROSES FOR MEDIUM HEDGES

'Ballerina' (Hybrid Musk, single, pink white center); 'Red Coat' (Modern Shrub, crimson scarlet); 'Windrush' (Modern Shrub, soft yellow).

ROSES FOR SHORT HEDGES

'Little White Pet' (Cluster-Flowered, white); 'Old Blush China' (China, pale pink); 'Rosa Mundi' (Gallica, crimson and white stripes).

Wichuraiana Rambler 'Evangeline' produces clusters of single creamy-pink flowers.

ROSES FOR IMPENETRABLE BARRIERS

'Cerise Bouquet' (modern shrub, cerise pink); 'Frühlingsgold' (*R. pimpinellifolia* hybrid, single yellow); 'Nevada' (*R. pimpinellifolia* hybrid, creamy white); 'Pink Surprise' (*R. bracteata* x *R. rugosa*, blush pink); *R. eglanteria* (pink); *R. rugosa* (white, red).

ROSES WITH ORNAMENTAL HIPS

'Eddie's Jewel' (*R. moyesii* hybrid, bright red); 'Frau Dagmar Hartopp' (Hastrup) (*R. rugosa*, clear pink); 'Hansa' (*R. rugosa*, red violet); *R. rugosa* 'Alba' (white); 'Scabrosa' (*R. rugosa*, crimson mauve).

OLD GARDEN ROSES TO GROW IN POTS

'Comte de Chambord' (Portland, blue pink); 'Etoile de Lyon' (Tea, gold yellow); 'Jacques Cartier' (Portland, clear pink); 'Perle d'Or' (China, cream yellow); 'Rose de Meaux' (Centifolia, soft pink).

MODERN GARDEN ROSES TO GROW IN POTS

'Amber Queen' (Cluster-Flowered, deep apricot); 'Festival' (dwarf Cluster-Flowered, scarlet); 'Fragrant Delight' (Cluster-Flowered, salmon pink); 'House Beautiful' (dwarf Cluster-Flowered, bright yellow); 'Royal William' (Large-Flowered, bright red); 'Sexy Rexy' (Cluster-Flowered, clear pink); Silver Jubilee' (Large-Flowered, apricot pink, darker edges).

CLASSIFICATION OF ROSES

The long history of rose breeding means that today's rose lovers can enjoy a huge variety of beautiful plants. We have come to expect a great deal from roses, and with careful choice and good cultivation they reward us with flowers from spring until the dark days of winter; scent that fills the summer garden and lingers on in oils, preserves and potpourri; decorative hips, leaves and even thorns. There are forms and styles suitable for nearly every situation, from diminutive Patio bushes to huge Ramblers cascading in luxurious swags from trees and arbors.

There are several thousand documented roses including original species and the scores of hybrids that have been cultivated during the last four centuries. New rose hybrids are being introduced every year in addition to older hybrids being rediscovered growing all over the world. In 1971, the World Federation of Rose Societies reclassified both ancient and modern roses into two separate groups.

Broadly speaking, the era of the modern rose began in 1867 with the introduction of the first "Hybrid Tea," 'La France'. The World Federation includes nineteen categories of modern garden roses and eighteen of old garden roses as well as groups for climbing and non-climbing species roses.

In some books you may still see the terms Hybrid Tea shrub (now Large-Flowered shrub), and Floribunda shrub (now Cluster-Flowered shrub). The small Patio bush roses have been renamed rather clumsily as Dwarf Cluster-Flowered bushes. There is still considerable debate concerning these classifications, and it is likely that terms such as "hybrid tea" will continue to be used by gardeners and professional growers alike.

Modern Garden Roses

CLIMBING

- Non-recurrent Flowering
  - Climbing Miniature
  - Climber
    - Cluster-Flowered
    - Large-Flowered
  - Rambler
- Recurrent Flowering
  - Miniature
  - Climber
    - Cluster-Flowered
    - Large-Flowered
  - Rambler

NON-CLIMBING

- Non-recurrent Flowering
  - Ground-cover
  - Shrub
    - Cluster-Flowered
    - Large-Flowered
- Recurrent Flowering
  - Miniature
  - Bush
    - Dwarf Cluster-Flowered
    - Polyantha
    - Cluster-Flowered
    - Large-Flowered
  - Shrub
    - Cluster-Flowered
    - Large-Flowered
  - Ground-cover

A traditional rose garden in full bloom is a pleasure to behold.

Fashions in garden design, as in clothes, are constantly changing – for example, since the turn of the century roses have been incorporated in herbaceous borders instead of being grown in separate beds. Modern Shrub roses are easy-to-grow bushes with rambler-like flowers which are either remontant or flower just once but over a long period. The most popular of modern roses are the Large-Flowered shrubs (Hybrid Teas) and Cluster-Flowered shrubs (Floribunda) which grow between about 24 inches and 4 feet tall. The smaller Patio and Miniature roses may be grown at the front of borders as well as in pots and tubs.

Modern Climbers are a relatively new group of climbing remontant roses. They are rather shorter in growth than older varieties – between 8 feet and 12 feet – but may be trained as pillar roses. Some modern varieties of roses also make natural hedges or may be used to disguise ugly fencing. Procumbent or Ground-cover roses are mostly low-maintenance plants which may be grown in containers as well as in rockeries or trailing over walls and down banks. Then there are the Climbers and the Ramblers, the former having more of an erect growth habit suitable for walls and the latter can be grown over pergolas and arbors, through bushes, into trees and to conceal unsightly tree stumps or the side of a shed. Finally, there are the English roses, although not a recognized modern category they do include some of the most popular contemporary roses with varieties small enough to fit into the tiniest garden and others like the ever popular 'Gertrude Jekyll', which grow to about 4 feet.

The following lists are by no means comprehensive, merely a selection of some of the more popular and successful varieties of each group divided into colors or shades. Whether a particular rose is suitable for your garden or its intended position needs further investigation.

Modern Garden Roses

SHRUBS

There is a great deal of diversity in this group as most of the roses are crosses between Modern Bushes and Climbers, which means

The beautiful pink tones of the Modern Shrub rose 'Angelica'.

that some of them are adaptable for climbing. They are strong and free-flowering.

Apricot, copper, orange: 'Autumn Sunset'; 'Bonn'; 'Fred Loads'; 'Grandmaster'; 'Joseph's Coat'.

Crimson, scarlet: 'Cardinal Hume'; 'Fountain'; 'La Sevillana'; 'Malcolm Sargent'; 'Red Coat'.

Lilac, mauve: 'Lavender Lassie'; 'Magenta'; 'Zigeunerknabe' ('Gipsy Boy').

Pink, blush: 'Angelica'; 'Armada'; 'Bonica '82'; 'Cerise Bouquet'; 'Dapple Dawn'; 'Kathleen Ferrier'.

White, cream: 'Jacqueline du Pré'; 'Little White Pet'; 'Pearl Drift'; 'Sally Holmes'; 'White Spray'.

Yellow, gold: 'Anna Zinkeisen'; 'Baby Love'; 'Goldbusch'; 'Golden Wings'; 'Lichtkönigin Lucia'.

LARGE-FLOWERED SHRUBS (HYBRID TEA)

Probably the most popular of all roses, members of this group have long pointed buds and flowers borne singly or in small clusters; many are highly scented. Their diverse color range combined with their long flowering period make these roses popular for growing in flower beds and borders.

Apricot, copper, orange: 'Doris Tysterman'; 'Julia's Rose'; 'Just Joey'; 'Lincoln Cathedral'; 'Whisky Mac'.

Crimson, scarlet: 'Alexander'; 'Josephine Bruce'; 'Madame Louis Laperrière'; 'National Trust'; 'Royal William'.

Lilac, mauve: 'Blue Moon'; 'Bleu Parfum'; 'Heirloom'; 'Intermezzo'; 'Rose Gaujard'.

Pink, blush: 'Blessings'; 'Paul Sherville'; 'Royal Highness'; 'Silver Jubilee'; 'Susan Hampshire'.

White, cream: 'Elizabeth Harkness'; 'Peaudouce'; 'Polar Star'; 'Pristine'; 'Virgo'.

A perfect example of the Hybrid Tea rose 'Alexander'.

'Bonica '82' is a vigorous, spreading Shrub rose with masses of pink flowers.

Yellow, gold: 'Grandpa Dickson'; 'King's Ransom'; 'Peace'; 'Sunblest'; 'Tequila Sunrise'.

CLUSTER-FLOWERED SHRUBS (FLORIBUNDA)

These shrubs flower practically non-stop throughout the summer and autumn and their clusters of informal nosegays or roses can be mixed successfully with other herbaceous perennials, small hedges and shrubs.

Apricot, copper, orange: 'Amber Queen'; 'Anne Harkness'; 'Apricot Nectar'; 'Fellowship'; 'Harvest Fayre'.

Crimson, scarlet: 'Beautiful Britain'; 'City of Belfast'; 'Europeana'; 'Evelyn Fison'; 'Lili Marlene'.

Lilac, mauve: 'Harry Edland'; 'Lavender Pinocchio'; 'Lilac Charm'; 'News'; 'Old Master'.

Pink, blush: 'Bonica '82'; 'English Miss'; 'Escapade'; 'Pink Parfait'; 'Sexy Rexy'.

White, cream: 'Evening Star'; 'Iceberg'; 'Margaret Merril'; 'St John'; 'Yvonne Rabier'.

Yellow, gold: 'Allgold'; 'Arthur Bell'; 'Golden Years'; 'Korresia'; 'Mountbatten'.

MINIATURE AND PATIO ROSES

This group encompasses Patio roses, dwarf Polyanthas and compact Polyanthas, which are ideal for very small gardens and for growing in tubs on patios and wind-protected balconies. Miniature roses grow to between 12 inches and 18 inches high and may be included in window-boxes or used as indoor pot plants throughout the year.

Apricot, copper, orange: 'Apricot Sunblaze' (Patio); 'Hula Girl' (Miniature); 'Orange

Rosa chinensis, the China rose, is an excellent Miniature rose suitable for containers.

'Grouse' is a trailing, Ground-cover rose with flat, single blush-pink flowers.

'Sunblaze' (Patio); 'Peek-a-Boo' (Patio); 'Sweet Dream' (Patio).

Crimson, scarlet: 'Festival' (Patio); 'Meillandina' (Patio); 'My Valentine' (Miniature); 'Red Ace' (Miniature); 'Wee Jock' (Patio).

Lilac, mauve: 'Baby Faurax' (Patio); 'Lavender Jewel' (Miniature); 'Lavender Sweetheart' (Miniature); 'Pink Posy' (Patio); 'Yesterday' (Patio).

Pink, blush: 'Dresden Doll' (Miniature); 'Gentle Touch' (Patio); 'Green Diamond' (Miniature); 'Queen Mother' (Patio); 'Yesterday' (Patio).

White, cream: 'Cinderella' (Miniature); 'Easter Morning' (Miniature); 'Pandora' (Miniature); 'Yorkshire Sunblaze' (Patio).

Yellow, gold: 'Baby Gold Star' (Miniature); 'Clarissa' (Patio); 'Pandora' (Miniature); 'Penelope Keith' (Patio); 'Perestroika' (Patio).

PROCUMBENT OR GROUND-COVER ROSES

These roses may be grown to form a blanket of color and provide dense and bushy shrubs. Varieties in this new group are proving very popular as they are hardy and disease-free.

Apricot, copper, orange: 'Sussex'.

Crimson, scarlet: 'Chilterns'; 'Fiona'; 'Hertfordshire'; 'Red Blanket'; 'Suffolk'.

Lilac, mauve: 'Laura Ashley'.

Pink, blush: 'Baroque'; 'Carefree Beauty'; 'Essex'; 'Pearl Drift'; 'Pink Bells'.

White, cream: 'Fairyland'; 'Francine'; 'Grouse'; 'Pleine de Grâce'; 'Snow Carpet'.

Yellow, gold: 'Norfolk'; 'Tall Story'.

CLIMBERS

These are really large shrubs which, if positioned by a wall or given a trellis for support, will grow like the old climbing roses, though not usually to the same size.

The beautiful climbing rose 'Bobbie James'.

'Aloha' is a modern climbing rose with full, double flowers.

Apricot, copper, orange: 'Alchemist'; 'Breath of Life'; 'Compassion'; 'Schoolgirl'; 'Warm Welcome'.

Crimson, scarlet: 'Altissimo'; 'Copenhagen'; 'Danse de Feu'; 'Dublin Bay'; 'Sympathie'.

Lilac, mauve: 'Ash Wednesday'; 'New Dawn'; 'Rosy Mantle'.

Pink, blush: 'Aloha'; 'Constance Spry'; 'Malaga'; 'Norwich Pink'; 'Pink Perpétue'.

White, cream: 'Bobbie James'; 'City of York'; 'Climbing Iceberg'; 'Ilse Krohn Superior'; 'Swan Lake'; 'White Cockade'.

Yellow, gold: 'Casino'; 'Golden Showers'; 'Highfield'; 'Laura Ford' (climbing Miniature); 'Night Light'.

RAMBLERS

This group consists mainly of hybrids of *R. wichuraiana*, a species with a low-growing habit which originates from Japan and Korea. It has flexible shoots which can grow up to

*The vigorous Rambler 'Blush Rambler' is a
particularly good scrambler.*

10–12 feet in one year. Other hybrids are from *R. sempervirens*, known as "the evergreen rose," *R. sinowilsonii*, *R. soulieana* and *R. setigera* whose hybrids are particularly popular in America, the most famous being 'Baltimore Belle.' They are very versatile and will ramble through bushes and up into trees or cover arches and pergolas.

Apricot, copper, orange: 'Auguste Gervais'; 'Léontine Gervais'; 'Madame Alice Garnier'; 'Paul Transon'; 'René André'.

Crimson, scarlet: 'Cadenza'; 'Chevy Chase'; 'Crimson Shower'; 'Dr Huey'; 'Excelsa'.

Lilac, mauve: 'Ethel'; 'Flora'; 'Minnehaha'; 'Rose Marie Viaud' (purple violet).

Pink, blush: 'Baltimore Belle'; 'Blush Rambler'; 'Evangeline'; 'New Dawn'; 'Kew Rambler'; 'Paul's Himalayan Musk'.

White, cream: 'Mountain Snow'; 'Long John Silver'; 'Sanders White'; 'Snowdrift';

Yellow, gold: 'Albéric Barbier'; 'Aviateur Blériot'; 'Emily Gray'; 'Jersey Beauty'; 'Lykkefund'.

ENGLISH ROSES

This is another group that falls into the category of modern garden roses as they have been bred relatively recently by David Austin Roses, near Wolverhampton, England. Though recurrent-flowering, they have the soft muted colors and all the wonderful fragrance of Old Roses, and are the result of marrying old varieties with modern Large- and Cluster-Flowered roses.

Apricot, copper, orange: 'Abraham Darby'; 'Ambridge Rose'; 'Evelyn'; 'Pat Austin'; 'Sweet Juliet'.

Crimson, scarlet: 'L.D. Braithwaite'; 'Noble Antony'; 'The Dark Lady'; 'The Herbalist'; 'The Prince'.

Lilac, mauve: 'Charles Rennie Mackintosh'; 'Cymbeline'; 'Lilac Rose'.

*The varying pink tones of 'The Herbalist'
adds to its charm.*

*The compact, exquisitely scented rose
'Charles Rennie Mackintosh'.*

Pink, blush: 'Brother Cadfael'; 'Eglantyne'; 'Gertrude Jekyll'; 'Heritage'; 'Mistress Quickly'.

White, cream: 'Fair Bianca'; 'Glamis Castle'; 'Moonbeam'; 'The Nun'; 'Winchester Cathedral'.

Yellow, gold: 'Charlotte'; 'Graham Thomas'; 'Happy Child'; 'Jayne Austin'; 'Pegasus.'

Old Garden Roses

The different groups of old garden roses reached the height of their popularity in the eighteenth and nineteenth centuries. Their magnificent scent compensates for their relatively short flowering season. You are unlikely to find many of these in your local supermarket or garden center but there are several rose specialists who still grow these old and in some cases ancient shrubs.

ALBAS

These are the white roses which were probably first introduced into Britain by the Romans. Many are shade-tolerant and can also cope with poor soils. Their foliage is usually gray-green and their colors range from soft pinks to creamy whites.

'Alba Maxima,' 'The Jacobite Rose' (pale blush tint); 'Celestial' (soft pink); 'Maiden's Blush' (blush pink); 'Madame Plantier' (capable of climbing, creamy white); 'Queen of Denmark' (soft pink); *R. alba* 'White Rose of York', 'Ayrshire' (*R. arvensis*).

RAMBLERS

This is a very small group of Ramblers and roses with a scrambling habit which are derived from the indigenous field rose in Scotland. These roses therefore tend to prefer a colder climate but have also been found

Arches of roses line a pebble path bordered by lavender.

in warmer climes such as California and Texas.

'Ayrshire Splendens' (purple tinted white); 'Dundee Rambler' (white); 'Düsterlohe' (single flower, red); 'Ruga' (pale pink); 'Venusta Pendula' (pink white).

BOURBONS AND CLIMBING BOURBONS

First appearing in the mid-nineteenth century, the Victorians revelled in the repeat-flowering habit of these hybrids. They were the result of crossing repeat-flowering China roses with Portland roses.

'Boule de Neige' (creamy white); 'Louise Odier' (warm pink); 'Madame Isaac Pereire' (purple crimson); 'Souvenir de la Malmaison' (soft pink); 'Vivid' (magenta pink); 'Zéphirine Drouhin' (climbing, cerise pink); 'Zigeunerknabe' (dark pink).

BOURSAULTS AND CLIMBING BOURSAULTS

These two small groups are roses with smooth stems and dark wood.

'Amadis' ('Crimson Boursault') (deep red); 'Blush Boursault' (climbing, blush pink); 'Madame Sancy de Parabère' (climbing, rich pink); 'Morletti' (magenta pink).

CHINAS

These roses first appeared in Europe in 1781 when a pink form of *R. chinensis* was planted in the Netherlands and another was found some years later growing in Calcutta. In temperate climates they rarely grow more than 4 feet but are free-flowering, particularly in a sunny site, protected from cold winds.

'Louis XIV' (very dark red); 'Old Blush' (pale pink deepening with age); 'Sophie's Perpetual' (dark pink); 'Viridiflora' (unusual green flowers).

Ramblers are perfect for scrambling over arches and pergolas.

'Zéphirine Drouhin' and Clematis 'Niobe', growing together in perfect harmony.

DAMASKS

This group is derived from *R. damascena*, named after Damascus. These roses found their way to Europe by means of the returning Crusaders and many of the surviving hybrids are pre-sixteenth century. They all have the distinctive damask perfume prized by perfumiers and apothecaries.

'Madame Hardy' (pure white); 'Marie Louise' (clear pink); 'Quatre Saisons' (clear pink); 'York and Lancaster' (striped and mottled pink).

GALLICAS

Probably the oldest cultivated rose, grown by both the Greeks and the Romans. These varieties make compact plants, perfect for small gardens, and include beautiful shades of crimson and purple among their wide range of colors. The Empress Josephine is said to have

The delicate Bourbon rose 'Zigeunerknabe'.

assembled a collection of over one hundred and fifty different Gallicas in her celebrated garden at Malmaison.

'Cardinal de Richelieu' (dark purple); 'Empress Josephine' (clear pink); *R. gallica officinalis*, 'The Apothecary's Rose', 'The Red Rose of Lancaster' (light crimson); *R. mundi* (crimson striped with white); 'Tuscany Superb' (crimson purple).

HYBRID PERPETUALS

Popular with both the Victorians and Edwardians, they have rather blowsy flowers but most have a perfume and will flower a second time in the autumn. There are some very good examples of red roses in this group.

'Baron Girod de l'Ain' (bright crimson); 'Duke of Edinburgh' (bright red); 'Général Jacqueminot' (clear red); 'Gloire de Ducher' (deep red); 'La Reine' (silver pink).

MOSSES

Of *centifolia* origin, the distinctive feature of this group is its mossed buds and stems. Moss roses were very popular with the Victorians.

'Common Moss' ('Old Pink Moss') (clear pink); 'Comtesse de Murinais' (blush pink); 'Little Gem' (light crimson); 'Shailer's White Moss' (white); 'William Lobb' (purple magenta).

NOISETTES

As the Portland and Bourbon roses were being

developed in Europe, so too were the Noisettes in America. These were a cross between a China rose and *R. moschata*, the Musk rose. Some of these shrubs make good short climbers .

'Blush Noisette' (lilac pink); 'Bouquet d'Or' (copper yellow); 'Crepuscule' (apricot); 'Duchess d'Auerstädt' (pale orange); 'Madame Alfred Carrière' (climber, pink white).

PORTLANDS

All these roses flower repeatedly or continuously and as well as being suitable as colorful bedding shrubs they may also be grown in pots.

'Arthur de Sansal' (purple crimson); 'Comte de Chambord' (lilac pink); 'Duchess of Portland' (clear red); 'Jacques Cartier' (clear pink); 'Rose de Roi' (red violet).

The popular Climber 'Madame Alfred Carrière'.

PROVENCE ROSES (CENTIFOLIAS)

Also known as "cabbage roses" because of their numerous petals. The sheer weight of their flowers tends to make their heads hang.

'Duc de Fitzjames' (deep pink to purple); 'Duchess de Rohan' (lavender pink); 'Juno' (blush pink); 'La Noblesse' (silver pink); 'Petit de Hollande' (pink); 'Tour de Malakoff' ('Blue Jack') (magenta purple).

SEMPERVIRENS (EVERGREEN ROSES)

These roses were favored by the Victorians because they retained their spectacular foliage through most winters. They are ideal for pergolas, arches and for training against trellis.

'Adélaide d'Orléans' (powder pink); 'Félicité et Perpétue' (creamy white); 'Princess Louise' (creamy blush pink); 'Spectabilis' (pale lilac pink).

SWEET BRIARS (EGLANTERIA OR PENZANCE BRIARS)

These vigorous shrubs are excellent for informal hedges; they have sharp thorns and produce masses of bright hips in late summer and autumn.

'Edith Ballenden' (single flowers, pale pink); 'Hebe's Lip' (white tinted red); 'Lady Penzance' (coppery-yellow tints); 'Magnifica' (purple red); 'Manning's Blush' (white); 'Meg Merrilees' (crimson); 'Amy Robsart' (rose-pink); *R. eglanteria* (sweet briar) (pale pink).

A thick hedge can be made with Rosa rugosa 'Roseraie de l'Hay'.

TEAS AND CLIMBING TEAS (BENGAL ROSES)

These roses became known as Tea roses because the first one to be imported in 1824 was said to have a fragrance resembling the tea brought in the same ships from Bengal.

'The Bride' (white); 'Dr Grill' (coppery pink); 'Lady Hillingdon' (also climber, gold yellow); 'Mons Tillier' (deep purple); 'Parks Yellow', the original Tea rose, (pale yellow); 'Tipsy Imperial Concubine' (clear pink).

"Wild" or Species Roses

These are species of the genus *Rosa* and the ancestors of the cultivated roses and can be divided into four groups in the areas of the northern hemisphere where they grow wild. Though roses are found thriving in the southern hemisphere, there is no evidence that they evolved naturally and it is probable that they were introduced by settlers.

American Wild Roses: *R. blanda* and *R. gymnocarpa* which both resemble the European dog rose; *R. carolina*; *R. foliolosa*, found further south and thorn-free; *R. nitida*; *R. palustris* (swamp rose); *R. virginiana*.

European Wild Roses : *R. arvensis* (field rose); *R. canina* (dog rose); *R. eglanteria* (eglantine rose or sweet briar); *R. gallica* and *R. moschata* which are both found around the Mediterranean coastline; *R. pimpinellifolia* (scotch briar); *R. villosa* (apple rose).

Middle Eastern and Eastern European Wild Roses : *R. centifolia* and *R. damascena*, both famous for their high yields of rose attar (rose oil); *R. foetida*, the only true yellow species.

Oriental and Asian Wild Roses: *R. banksiae*, a thornless rose with flowers in clusters; *R. bracteata* and *R. laevigata*, both climbing roses with large white single flowers and nasty thorns; *R. filipes* and *R. moyesii* which have bottle-shaped hips; *R. chinensis*; *R. rugosa*, a popular species and hybrids for providing thick hedges; *R. wichuraiana*, a parent of some of the best Ramblers.

ROSES AND COMBINED PLANTINGS

Roses can be grown with most other garden plants, and although they prefer a clay-based or heavier soil, good preparation and regular feeding will ensure the best results in other types of soil. Carefully selected foliage plants and shrubs can provide a sympathetic palette for your chosen rose color. It is worth considering planting a couple of shrubs with foliage that will coordinate well with your roses for indoor arrangements. The tones of flowering perennials and annuals need to enhance the roses when they are in flower, rather than compete with them.

WHITE AND CREAM SHRUB ROSES

Gray, blue and soft green foliage, and

A pergola entwined with 'Wedding Day' and 'Bleu Magenta' roses above a huge clump of Nepeta (catmint).

'Penelope' is a fragrant hybrid musk rose which blends perfectly with Digitalis (foxglove) 'Suttons Apricot'.

flowering shrubs are ideal with white and cream roses. The following would combine well: *Ceanothus* 'Snowball', a white-flowered variety of this Californian lilac, also the blue variety 'Blue Mound'; *Cistus cyprius*, another white-flowered variety of the sun rose; *Deutzia*, which has bell-like flowers in white, and shades of pink and red; *Hebe*, the evergreen shrubs from New Zealand, particularly *H. pinguifolia* 'Pagel', which has gray-green leaves and white flowers, and other varieties with blue and pale lilac flowers; *Hydrangea paniculata grandiflora*, spectacular with clusters of white flowers; some white

varieties of fuchsia such as *Fuchsia magellanica* 'Alba' whose drooping bell-like flowers contrast well with rose shapes, as does the white variety of *Cytisus* (broom). *Lavandula* (lavender) is a very popular companion for roses and may be grown in clumps at the front of a border or trimmed into dwarf aromatic hedges. Suitable perennials include white *Gypsophila* (baby's breath); *Geranium* (the cranesbill types such as *G. clarkei*, 'Kashmir White' and *G. traversii elegans* 'Crug Strain'); silver, feathery *Artemisia* 'Powis Castle' and gray woolly leaved *Stachys olympica* (lamb's ears) and taller blue and lilac flowers such as *Scabiosa* (pincushion flower), *Lupinus* (lupine), *Iris* and the distinctive *Eryngium* (sea holly).

BLUSH, PINK AND DEEP RED SHRUB ROSES

These roses range from almost white to the soft warm pinks that are more blue than the fiery salmon tones and finally into the darker, deeper maroons and purple-reds. Good companions are shrubs such as red and pink *Berberis thunbergii* varieties; *Buddleja davidii* 'Harlequin' (butterfly bush) with its fragrant purple-red flower spikes; *Cotinus* 'Grace' (smoke bush) which has broad dark pink leaves and purple-pink flowers; *Viburnum*

The Bourbon rose 'Madame Isaac Pereire' has large, almost purple-pink blooms that are exquisitely perfumed.

tinus 'Eve Price,' an evergreen that has fragrant pink flowers in winter, and the pink-flowered varieties of *Weigela*. Suitable perennials include *Delphinium, Diascia* (twinspur), *Digitalis* (foxglove), some of the numerous pink varieties of hardy *Geranium* (cranesbill), *Phlox* and, for contrasting shape, the feathery pink and lilac varieties of *Astilbe*. *Dianthus* (garden pinks) have a strong peppery scent which blends well with the scent of roses, and blush and pink lilies are taller perfumed plants to consider.

YELLOW, COPPER AND SCARLET SHRUB ROSES

Quite the opposite from the cool white roses, these are dramatic and lively colors, but too much of them can be quite overpowering and

a considerable amount of green and variegated foliage is needed. *Choisya ternata* (Mexican orange blossom) has bright yellow leaves, so too have *Escallonia laevis* and some *Ilex* (holly). *Potentilla* (cinquefoil) is a small shrub – *P. fruticosa* 'Red Robin' has bright brick red flowers and *P. f.* 'Goldstar' bright yellow. *Pyracantha* (firethorn) is a hardy shrub bearing clusters of orange or red berries in the autumn; another berry-making shrub is *Hypericum* (St John's wort) – both the variegated and simple green varieties have bright yellow flowers and red or yellow fruits. Among perennial plants there is the florists' favorite, *Alchemilla mollis* (lady's mantle), which is perfect for bouquets and vase arrangements, with yellow-green foliage like many of the *Euphorbias* (spurge), a group of plants that is extremely fashionable and perfect with yellow and orange. *Kniphofias* (red hot pokers), yellow and red *Papaver* (poppies), *Rudbeckia* (cone flowers) and *Hemerocallis* (day-lilies) all have fine, dramatically contrasting shapes, whereas *Solidago* (golden rod) and *Saxifraga* (saxifrage) have more feathery shaped flowers.

CLIMBING AND RAMBLING ROSES

Clematis and roses have long been climbing companions. As the roses will need pruning in early spring, it is wise to choose a clematis that needs cutting back at the same time. These include large-flowered clematis such as

'Comtesse de Bouchard' (mauve pink) or 'Jackmanii' (deep violet); the smaller-headed *C. viticella* 'Etoile Violette' (violet) and 'Alba Luxurians' (white), plus the sweetly scented *C. thunbergii* which has small white flowers.

Some clematis cannot tolerate a north-facing wall but *C. campaniflora*, which has pale violet bell-shaped flowers, is happy growing on a north wall and could be grown with those roses that can take a northerly aspect such as 'Madame Alfred Carrière' (Noisette), 'Emily Gray' (*Wichuraiana* Rambler), and 'Aimée Vibert' (Noisette).

Another scented climber to grow with roses is *Lonicera*: *L. fragrantissima* has scented flowers in winter while *L. periclymenum* 'Belgica' flowers in early summer and 'Serotina' flowers later and into autumn.

'Gruss an Teplitz', a China rose with crimson blooms contrasts with red and yellow Aquilegia (columbines).

Buying, Planting, Feeding and Care

If the successful growing of roses takes skill so too does the designing of a satisfactory scheme that considers the available soil, size of garden and prevailing climate. The weather can vary dramatically from one year to the next, changing the color and frequency of your roses as well as their height and spread.

Roses do prefer clay-based, heavy soils if they are to flourish, and those grown on poorer and lighter soils may never reach their true potential without careful soil preparation and regular feeding. Albas, Gallicas, Damasks, Centifolias, Portlands and Moss roses can cope with less fertile soils, and so can the Shrub roses such as *R. rugosa*, *R. pimpinellifolia*,

Right: The delicate blue tones of the delphiniums perfectly offset the pale pink blooms of 'Comte de Chambord' in this lovely garden setting.

Below: Plant roses next to a stone wall for a delightful contrast between the hard-edged stonework and the blowsy rose blooms.

PLANTING A BARE-ROOT ROSE

"Bare-root" plants are dispatched in the lifting season, when the roses are dormant. It is wise to choose a nursery recognized by the ARS (American Rose Society) as its members will have standards of quality and service which offer a guarantee to the consumer. Orders need to be made by mid-summer if the roses are to arrive in time for an early planting. Before planting, prepare the soil as outlined below.

1 *If the plants are delivered during a severe, frosty spell when the ground is too hard for planting, keep their protective wrapping on and leave somewhere protected, like a shed or garage until the ground softens again.*

2 *A bush, shrub or old-fashioned rose requires a hole large enough to take the roots comfortably without any restriction. Scatter a handful of bonemeal at the bottom of the hole to promote root growth.*

3 *Add more bonemeal to the soil that will surround the plant. Gradually fill the hole around the rose, shaking the plant to ensure that soil falls between the roots and to eliminate any air pockets.*

4 *Step gently around the base of the plant to hold the rose tight but without compacting the soil. Make sure the base or "union" of the rose is completely covered with soil, because exposed "eyes" may result in suckers growing.*

R. eglanteria and their hybrids. Many of the climbing roses and Ramblers will also thrive, particularly those planted to scramble up trees.

Ideally, roses prefer soil with a pH of around 6.5, which is slightly acid, or neutral. If you are in any doubt about the pH level in your garden, it is wise to do a soil test using one of the kits readily available at garden centers. A well-prepared soil will reap rewards from your roses later and digging over the proposed site, mixing the existing soil with some organic material, is essential. Well-rotted farmyard manure is perfect but not readily available for most gardeners; well-rotted compost does just as well or, failing that, a mixture of bonemeal and one of the peat alternatives such as pulverized tree bark or coconut fiber.

If you have recently moved or are preparing a part of the garden that has not been cultivated previously, it is wise to dig a small trench at least 24 inches deep to ascertain the quality of the soil beneath root level. You may find a layer of compacted soil which will result in poor root growth and the possibility of the roses drowning because of inadequate drainage, or alternatively dying of thirst because the roots cannot penetrate through the compacted earth. It is better to avoid places where there is competition from other plants, particularly under trees where rainwater can drip onto rose leaves. If other roses have recently been grown on the site, replace the top soil with some from elsewhere in the garden to avoid the rose-sickness syndrome. Avoid windy places and those areas where frost collects such as the base of slopes.

Once you have chosen the position and decided which rose is most appropriate for that spot, you need to find the best means of buying your rose. There are basically three ways: direct from the nursery, usually by mail order; container-grown plants either from garden centers or specialist growers and plants from shops and supermarkets.

The first method is by far the most popular.

Rose heads in full bloom, luxuriating in the summer sun.

Container-grown roses are those most commonly found in garden centers, though many specialists also offer a selection of plants. These are available in the spring and summer months when they are often in flower so you can see what you are buying. The one disadvantage is that the choice is usually very limited as it would be impossible to stock all the many hundreds of varieties that are currently being bred. The plants sold in shops or supermarkets look like twigs often coated in wax, and tied in a plastic bag. Almost certainly

PLANTING A ROSE IN A CONTAINER

1 *If you are planting a Patio or Miniature rose in a pot, good drainage provided by crocks is essential, and you should use a reputable brand of potting soil. The size of the pot is important: it needs to be as high as the rose itself to provide adequate support and wide enough to give space around the roots for reasonable growth.*

2 *Wear protective gloves before carefully removing the plant from its container and gently easing out the roots. Take great care not to pull too hard on the roots as you may cause irreparable damage to your rose. Place a shallow layer of potting mix over the drainage crocks and place the rose centrally in the pot.*

3 *Fill the pot with soil to within 1 inch of its rim and press down firmly, making sure there are no air pockets anywhere. Water in thoroughly.*

4 *From time to time potted roses need repotting and this is ideally done in the dormant season, taking care not to disturb the root ball.*

there is a glossy picture showing brightly colored roses on the packaging. Be wary of these plants, as unless they are marked with a sell-buy date, they may well have been sitting on a warm shelf for weeks which encourages premature growth.

PRUNING AND CARE OF ROSES

There is much debate about the pruning of roses and the conflicting opinions and lengthy tomes on the subject could well put gardeners off growing roses at all! Pruning should not be confused with either cutting or dead-heading. Cutting flowers for decoration has no ill effect on a plant provided it is strong and healthy and, in the case of newly planted rose bushes, not too many leaves are removed. Avoid taking more than a third of a flowering stem, making the cut just above an outward-facing bud. Removing dead flower heads – dead-heading – is important because it conserves the energy the plant would otherwise use to produce hips and so encourages new flowering shoots. Obviously this procedure is not necessary for once-flowering roses or those grown for their decorative hips.

Pruning is the means by which a gardener cuts away any dead stock on the bush, to improve its shape and increase the light and air circulation in its center to ensure its good health. Poor light and lack of air will put the plant under stress, which makes it more prone to insect invasion and disease. The only requirements for pruning are a pair of really sharp pruners with a clean cutting edge and a pair of thick gardening gloves for comfort and protection.

The first real winter frosts will often destroy all the remaining blooms and buds.

Newly planted roses need hard pruning and, as they are most often planted in the spring, preferably before the last frost. This ensures that all the new shoots will grow from the bottom of the plant rather than the top and a stronger bush will grow as a result. For established rose bushes early spring is recommended for pruning, just as the plants are beginning to wake up from their dormant period. If they are pruned in the autumn or winter, a bitter frost can easily attack the open "wound," killing that part of the branch and causing it to die back. But if a bush is misshapen or straggly, a superficial prune to tidy it up will do no harm provided there is little chance of frost in the subsequent weeks. Ramblers often need some autumn pruning owing to their prolific summer growth, and old flowering stems may be cut to allow the new stems to develop flowers the following year. Climbers may also need trimming if they are taking up too much space or are becoming bare at the base of the plant.

Wind-rock is a common cause of roses failing to thrive, because the roots become loosened through the plant being continually moved about in the wind. Autumn pruning can eliminate this problem by cutting back any long and ungainly branches.

It is the general consensus that it is better to prune hard or not at all, preferably at the end of the roses' dormant period, making a clean cut just above an outward-facing bud. At about this time the roses are ready for feeding and a well-balanced fertilizer applied as a top dressing should be lightly raked in around each bush when the soil is moist.

Very little can go wrong with roses provided

the plants are healthy when they are planted, preferably not where other roses have been previously grown unless the top soil has been replaced. Roses like a good, well-drained soil and prefer not to be overcrowded. They need regular feeding in the growing period.

One advantage of frequent dead-heading is that a problem is quickly noticed before any real damage has occurred. Inspect the base of the plant too because this is where shoots grow from the rootstock rather than the variety grafted onto it. Known as suckers, they can easily take over the plant and should be removed by pulling each one off at the point of origin on the root. Snipping off suckers above ground level only encourages more to grow.

As for diseases, the most serious fungi are mildew, black spot and rust. Rust starts as orange swellings on the underside of leaves and new shoots often turn red and shrivel. It can be caused by shortage of potash in the soil and also by very dry weather followed by exceptional cold. Mildew is quite common and creates a white powdery mold on the leaves,

Both 'Bobbie James' (left) and 'American Pillar' are vigorous ramblers.

generally in summer or autumn. Dry roots, poor feeding and hot sun followed by cold nights are often the cause. Black spot is dreaded by rose-growers and again is probably owing to potash shortage and a warm, wet summer. It is difficult to control and all affected leaves should be removed.

None of these fungal diseases need be fatal and if caught early should respond to treatment by recommended systemic fungicides. There are of course many insects that enjoy feasting

on juicy rose leaves and insecticides are frequently combined with fungicides in commercial rose treatments. Systemic insecticides are particularly effective as they enter the sap stream, protecting new leaves and branches, and even insects hidden from the spraying cannot escape. Roses near a lawn can be damaged by weed-killer; to prevent this, choose a still day to treat the lawn and use a different watering can to water the roses.

Discolored or stunted leaf growth can be caused by a mineral shortage of some sort. Taking a couple of leaf samples to a reputable rose-grower or garden center is the safest way to obtain an accurate diagnosis and prescribed remedy.

If your garden suffers from prolonged and deep frosts, then some winter protection may be necessary. Obviously it is wise to select less tender roses but a protective blanket wrapped around each plant will prevent any damage; this should be removed once the new growing shoots have started and the danger of severe frost has passed.

1 Hard pruning is recommended for newly planted roses and it is essential to use a pair of really sharp pruners to ensure a clean cut.

2 Stems are cut back to about four or five buds from the bottom of the plant and this should leave short, strong stems of between 3–6 inches high.

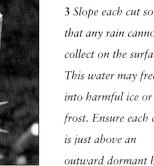

3 Slope each cut so that any rain cannot collect on the surface. This water may freeze into harmful ice or frost. Ensure each cut is just above an outward dormant bud.

37

CARE AND CONDITIONING OF CUT ROSES

Whether you are buying cut roses or taking them from the garden, always choose those in the very best condition. Reputable florists, supermarkets and flower stalls take pride in their flowers, selling only good-quality blooms and having the knowledge and experience to keep them that way.

If you are cutting roses from the garden, it is best to do this first thing in the morning, when their water content is highest. Cut the flowers at a sharp angle just above a leaf node, and be sure not to be so greedy that you rob each bush of all its blooms or destroy its overall appearance! Place the flowers immediately in a bucket of water, where they can have a long drink.

If you are buying roses, make sure they are well wrapped to avoid excess evaporation and to protect their delicate petals. For long journeys it is better to put them in a bucket of water but if this is impractical, ask the retailer to cover the stem ends with damp paper. Once home, give the flowers a long drink in deep tepid water.

Before arranging the flowers, always cut off any foliage that will fall below the water line in the container or vase. Make a long, diagonal cut from the bottom of each stem as this will provide the maximum area for water intake. Rose stems should never be crushed with a

As a gift, lay a bunch of roses and foliage diagonally on a square of paper and fold around the stems. Tie securely with raffia or ribbon.

1 *Always place roses in a bucket of tepid water for a couple of hours after purchase or cutting.*

hammer as so many books advocate. It has been proved by independent research that this method destroys the delicate plant cells and makes the stalk less efficient in taking up water; it also encourages bacterial infection.

Bacteria block the stems and cause the drooping heads so often experienced with store-bought roses. You can avoid this problem by always using scrupulously clean vases, removing all leaves below the water level and adding commercially formulated flower food. This simple powder contains the correct amount of a mild and completely harmless disinfectant, which inhibits bacterial growth, together with a sugar that feeds the roses and encourages the flowers to mature

2 *After choosing the vase, cut off any leaves that will fall below the water level, because these will rot and stagnate the water.*

3 *Using a very sharp knife or pair of pruners, cut the stem diagonally to ensure maximum water uptake.*

4 *If thorns have to be removed because the roses are being used in a bouquet, use pruners or shears to cut them off, but not too close to the stem.*

5 *Add a commercially prepared flower food to the water in the vase in order to prolong the life of cut flowers and help to keep the vase water clear.*

6 *It is sometimes possible to revive wilted roses by cutting the heads very short.*

7 *Give first aid to wilting flower heads by wrapping in paper and standing in plenty of water.*

and open. If flower food is added to the water it is unnecessary to change it, though it may need topping up in warm weather. Although many people have their own recipes for increasing roses' longevity – lemonade, aspirins, household bleach and so on – flower food is by far the most successful way of keeping roses at their best for longer.

If rose heads have wilted, and this may be a result of bacterial infection or an airlock somewhere in the stem, it may be possible to revive them by wrapping them in strong paper

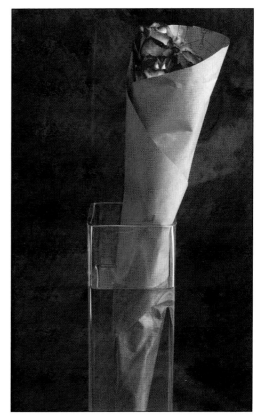

and standing the stems in tepid water up to their heads for several hours after first cutting at least 2 inches from the end of each stem. Sometimes even more drastic action is needed and the roses will have to be cut very short in order to perk up their drooping heads.

Finally, there are many theories about rose thorns. Again, research has proved that bacteria may invade the gashes left in the stem when thorns are cut off, so this should be done only if the roses are being used in a bouquet or nosegay where thorns could prick the hands.

DRYING ROSES

Roses have been dried for as long as they have been cultivated; their petals have been used in potpourri or the whole stems in decorative arrangements when the fresh flowers were scarce. The Elizabethans preserved roses by immersing them completely in dry sand and keeping them warm until all the moisture had been drawn out. In Victorian times, when houses were heated with open coal fires, which shortens the lives of fresh blooms, intricate dried arrangements were painstakingly created and then covered in glass domes to keep them dust-free. These somewhat tortured, contrived designs have long since lost their appeal in preference for looser, more natural arrangements and contemporary designs using dried flowers have gained a new popularity.

There are three principal ways of drying roses: in the air, in a microwave oven and using a desiccant. The latest commercial method is freeze-drying. This successful technique was originally developed as a means to store penicillin and blood plasma during the Second World War. It requires specialized freezers so it is no use putting a bunch of roses in a domestic model. The process can take up to two weeks and is therefore very expensive, but the results are stunning, producing dried roses with all their former intensity of color and in some cases even preserving their perfume. Flowers or bouquets dried by this method can allegedly last for about five years before they start to fade or disintegrate.

Air-drying is the most common method and by far the cheapest as it requires no more than the cost of the roses. This method is best for rose buds that are just about to open but still have their bud shape. They need to be hung somewhere warm, dry and dark with good ventilation for a couple of weeks – a large airing-cupboard may be ideal. Stringing them together washing-line style speeds up the process and prevents any moisture being trapped between the flowers which may

The easiest way to dry roses is to hang them upside down in a dark, warm and well-ventilated room.

*Once the roses are
completely dry, carefully
strip off the leaves and tie
the buds tightly together.
Dry stems are quite brittle
and binding them closely
into a compact bunch
gives them more stability.
Combined with a halo of
dried lavender, a small
nosegay in a terra-cotta
pot makes a delightful gift.*

DESICCANT DRYING

Desiccant-drying using silica gel crystals or fine sand may be used for fully open roses. Silica is available from some larger pharmacies.

1 *Put ½ inch of the crystals or sand in an airtight container and lay the rose heads face up.*

2 *Cover very carefully with more sifted desiccant until every part of the flower is concealed. Then seal the container and keep at room temperature for approximately seven to ten days before removing from the desiccant.*

develop into mildew. Once they are completely dry, handle them with care as the stems are very brittle. A tight bunch of rose buds packed together in a small terra-cotta pot will give added impact to the now faded color of the petals. A gentle blow on the lowest setting of a hair drier usually removes most of any dust.

As the flowers need to fit the radius of the turntable, microwave-drying is suitable only for arrangements requiring quite short stems. Lay the flowers on waxed paper and put into the microwave oven on the lowest setting. The roses need to be checked every minute to prevent "overcooking."

Roses in the Home

Gather therefore the rose,

whilst yet is prime.

EDMUND SPENCER (1553-1599)

TABLE STYLING WITH ROSES

Even the simplest meal may be transformed into something quite special with the addition of a few beautiful flowers onto the table. In summer when garden roses are plentiful it takes only a few to add scent to a table setting. The strongest perfume comes from those that are in full bloom. Their heavy heads need to be cut short and may need the support of some other foliage such as lavender or rosemary.

Commercially grown roses are usually sold in bud so buy them a few days before they are needed to ensure that the roses open to produce large clusters of small flower heads that are perfect for low arrangements. Floral designs for tables are best kept short so diners can see across the table and plates may be passed without any obstacles. Alternatively, tall candelabra may be decorated with delicate foliage with rose heads wired to the candle holders. A piece of florists' foam fitted around the base of each candle can be easily concealed with foliage and short stems of roses gently pushed into it.

For special parties, a rose tucked inside a napkin ring for each guest is a personal welcome. Coordinating the color of the flower with the food and table linen looks stylish and professional. A table centerpiece of floating candles and roses is a simple idea for dinner parties and can be particularly attractive if both the roses and candles are sweetly scented. According to the ancient Romans, the addition of some fragrant rose petals to the wine delayed the intoxication of its drinkers! A bottle of sparkling white wine or rosé decanted into a large glass pitcher and then sprinkled with petals is a delightful way of serving this drink – or follow the recipe for Rose Petal Punch on page 111.

'Felicia' is one of the finest of the Hybrid Musk roses and three or four blooms arranged with a few sprigs of rosemary in a small glass inside a terra-cotta pot make a natural table setting. Commercially grown 'Baccarole' roses take several days to open fully and their blue-crimson color needs only a few campanula leaves to create a rich luxurious decoration for the table.

The late and very great grower Edward B. LeGrice of North Walsham, England, bred this delicious rose 'Josephine Bruce' in 1949. As roses are often named after famous people, it is usually possible to find one with the same or a similar first name and this makes a very personal and romantic gesture for a special occasion or birthday.

A couple of 'Peppermint Ice' garden roses tucked inside a napkin ring add an extravagant finishing touch. As a souvenir for wedding guests, the chosen rose could be one of the same variety carried by the bride in her bouquet.

'Brown Velvet' is a modern Cluster-Flowered rose produced by Sam McGredy, a reputable Irish grower who moved his nursery from Portadown to New Zealand. Many of his roses have found their way back to the northern hemisphere. This dark brown red rose makes a perfect accompaniment to a plate of rich luscious strawberries and its cluster form requires just a couple of stems to fill a small vase.

ROSE AND FRUIT BASKET

For a special dinner party or to decorate a buffet table, this ornate moss-covered basket could contain either commercially grown or garden roses. Whichever roses you choose, it is important to select a sympathetically colored fruit or berry that will enhance the flowers. The 'Prelude' rose is a commercially grown scented rose, and its delightful lilac tone is perfectly coordinated here with branches of small, immature purple plums and darker elderberry fronds. Crimson rose hips and crab apples would look stunning arranged with red, orange or yellow roses, but for roses with a cream and white coloring, green fruits or vegetables such as greengage plum and baby artichokes would create a more attractive, striking result.

Dried poppy heads make a good contrast in shape to the roses. Alternatively, wired pine cones, either naturally colored or lightly sprayed with gold or silver, could be used to add a festive appearance to an arrangement.

*piece of florists' foam
cut to fit snugly in
the plastic bowl
plastic bowl
string
several handfuls of
moss
wire basket*

*wooden skewer
selection of small
branches with small
plums and
elderberry fruits
6 poppy heads
8 roses
3 beeswax candles*

WARNING: Never leave lit candles unattended, even for a few minutes.

1 *Soak the foam in water until it is completely saturated. Wedge into the bowl and secure with string if the fit is not tight. Arrange the moss around the bowl to conceal it within the basket.*

2 *Make random holes in the foam with a wooden skewer to accommodate the branches and roses. If you push a rose stem straight into the foam, it is probable that particles of foam will get lodged in the base of the stem and prevent good water uptake, causing premature wilting.*

3 *Make the initial shape of the arrangement using just the foliage and poppy heads. Finally, place the roses randomly, turning the basket to see the effect from all sides. Avoid putting the roses too close together. Then place the candles securely, making sure that no foliage or flowers are near the flames.*

Left: Beeswax candles smell wonderful as they burn and also tend to last longer than paraffin wax candles.

Below: Rose heads are less fragile and easier to manipulate when they are in buds. Always allow enough space in an arrangement for the bloom to be able to open fully without disrupting the other flowers or fruits.

47

POTPOURRI

In times when standards of personal hygiene weren't as high as today's, and rubbish was thrown from windows onto the street, scented flowers and plants were essential to mask the vile odors of everyday life. Dried herbs were burned in fireplaces to stave off the dreaded plague and floors were covered with branches of fragrant lavender, rosemary, sage and other aromatic herbs. Bowls were filled with dried scented roses to sweeten the air and different blends using a range of perfumed flowers were used to create a floral scent for each room.

The name "potpourri" means, literally, rot-pot, and the moist method of making the mixture involves mushing together petals and spices with salt and sometimes brandy and leaving in a jar for a week. The dry method is simpler and the results are more attractive. To make quantities of potpourri, you need to grow – as well as roses – lavender, scented *Pelargonium* (geranium), *Dianthus* (garden

pinks) and other brightly colored flowers such as *Delphinium*, *Calendula* (marigold) and herbs such as borage, lemon balm, chamomile, mint and lemon verbena.

Orris root is required in both moist and dry potpourri recipes. This is a powdered root that acts as a fixative in these scented blends and is available from traditional pharmacists and herbalists.

Lay freshly picked rose petals and leaves on blotting paper or other absorbent paper, making sure that the petals are not touching. Let dry in a cool place where there is a good flow of air. Sprays of flowers like delphiniums need to have their individual flower heads removed from the stem. Use only when the petals are completely dry.

Above: Petals and rose heads need to be left somewhere cool and dry with a good air flow.

Left: Potpourri may be enhanced by adding a few drops of rose essential oil or the less expensive rose geranium oil, or one of the synthetic potpourri refreshers which intensify the rose perfume.

Rose and Delphinium Potpourri

9 oz dried scented rose petals
3½ oz dried delphinium flowers and marigold petals
1 tbsp dried mint leaves
1 tsp ground cloves
1 tsp ground cinnamon
1 tsp ground allspice
1 tbsp orris root
8 drops rose essential oil

Mix the petals and flowers together in a large screw-topped jar, adding each of the other ingredients one by one. Shake well in between each addition. Screw the lid on tightly and let sit for two to three days in a dark cupboard.

Citrus and Rose-scented Potpourri

9 oz dried scented rose petals
3½ oz dried lavender and lemon balm
dried grated peel of 2 large lemons
1 tsp allspice
1 tsp orris root

Mix the flowers and herbs together in an airtight container, add the lemon peel and let sit for two to three days. Add the spice and orris root, shake well, and let sit for a week, stirring occasionally.

When the petals are completely dry, they are ready to be made into potpourri.

Elizabethan Moist Potpourri

about 2¼ lb fresh scented rose petals
¾ cup sea salt
3 tbsp ground allspice
2 tbsp ground cloves
3 tbsp brown sugar
4 tbsp orris root powder
1 tbsp brandy
½ oz fresh lavender flowers
½ oz fresh lemon verbena leaves
½ oz fresh scented Pelargonium *leaves*

Mix the rose petals and the salt together. Seal the container and let sit for three to four days. Transfer the petals into a large bowl and add the remaining ingredients, one by one, stirring well. Cover and stir the mixture every couple of days for two weeks using a wooden spoon. After about three weeks decant the moist mixture into jars with perforated lids.

SCENTED LACE CUSHION AND SACHETS

Making this cushion could not be simpler – it requires no sewing at all, just a safety pin! The lace is fine enough to allow the rose petal scent to permeate a clothes drawer or a pile of pillows on a bed. From time to time a little essential oil or potpourri refreshing perfume will be needed to refresh the petals. Tiny sachets can also be made from circles of the thinnest muslin or by using  lace handkerchiefs. Make a small pile of potpourri in the center of the fabric, crushing or tearing some of the larger petals or rose heads. Gather the fabric together and tie securely with a fine ribbon. Small silk or fabric rose buds or flowers may then be sewn or glued to the neck of the bag. If you are making a present of some fine linen or lingerie, the addition of two or three rose sachets makes more of your gift.

lace or fine synthetic
lace curtain fabric,
10 x 10 in
pins
1 yd each of two
colors of thin silk

ribbon
safety pin
sharp scissors
rose-scented
potpourri

Scented sachets may be made from lace handkerchiefs that are simply tied up with a piece of ribbon.

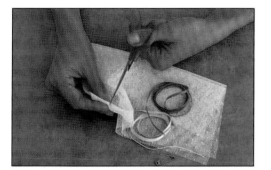

1 *Fold the fabric in half and pin the edges together. Make small cuts through both pieces of fabric ¾ in from the edge and at small intervals all around the oblong.*

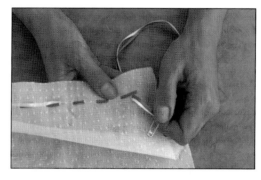

2 *Attaching one end of both pieces of ribbon to the safety pin, thread it through the holes, leaving a small gap on one side of the cushion for filling with potpourri.*

3 *Fill the cushion with rose-scented potpourri through the small opening. Crush or tear the larger petals or rose heads to fit through the small opening.*

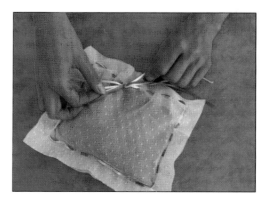

4 *When the cushion is filled, continue threading the ribbon, cut to length and tie in a bow. If you pull the ribbon tight, you can give the hem a gathered effect.*

ROSE-SCENTED BAGS

A translucent, gossamer fabric made into a simple bag and filled with scented rose heads and petals is a delightfully feminine idea for a guest room. Keep the flowers lightly perfumed by adding a few drops from a small bottle of potpourri refresher. Larger bags with a drawstring hung in a wardrobe will emit a faint but pleasant aroma each time the door is opened. You could make an alternative to a Christmas stocking by filling a large version with dried rose petals and tiny gifts. Choose fabric that is either extremely fine or transparent such as organza, fine silk and chiffon or open-weave linen or muslin that will allow the perfumed flowers to breathe through it.

materials to make a
bag approximately
6 x 8 in
outer fabric, 6 x 8 in
lining fabric
pins

length of
coordinating color
cord, about 16 in
adhesive tape
2 matching tassels
dried scented rose
petals

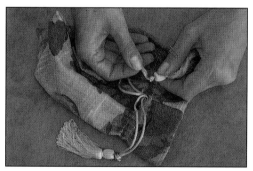

1 *Lay the two pieces of fabric one on top of the other, right sides together. Sew a seam around all four sides, leaving a 1¼ in gap on one side. Turn the bag through this gap so that it is right side out. Press all four seams and slip stitch the small gap closed. About one-quarter of the way down the bag run two lines of stitches across the width of the bag, about ¾ in apart. This is to accommodate the drawstring. Fold the bag along its side seams with the right sides together. Sew up the bottom and side of the bag. Turn right sides out and press.*

2 *At the side seam, make a small snip in the outer fabric to allow the drawstring through. Take care not to cut through both sets of fabric. Wind a piece of adhesive tape around the end of the cord to prevent it from fraying and feed it into the gap in the seam. Feed it all the way around the bag and out at the other side through another small hole. Tie a single loop in both ends of the cord and attach a matching tassel to the end of each cord.*

3 *Fill the bag with scented rose petals. Pull the cord to create gathers in the neck of the bag. Tie a knot to secure the bag and neaten any edges.*

A few drops of rose essential oil will refresh the petals and keep the rose bags fragrant.

ROSE CANDLES

Candlelight is still the most romantic and flattering artificial light you can create. It enhances food, cunningly hides any dust or flaws in the room and makes faces look warm and glowing. Scented candles imbue a gentle fragrance as they burn, but you should buy the better-quality examples as cheaper versions use synthetic and often overpowering scents. A few drops of essential oil may be added to the melted pool of wax as the candle is burning for the same effect.

Aromatic burners give you the option of mixing different oils together or varying the oil if you so desire. A purpose-made dish is gently warmed by a nightlight underneath, and as the oil evaporates, it releases its fragrance into the surrounding atmosphere. A homemade version can be improvized by placing drops of essential oil in a saucer and leaving it on top of a warm radiator.

Decorating plain candles is easy to do and the effect can be stunning. Rose heads and leaves are easy to apply as decoration and each time the candle is dipped a layer of melted wax seals the flower or leaf more deeply into the candle. Heavier objects take more practice, since speed is crucial if the decoration is to stick before the wax hardens.

deep narrow
 saucepan
church candle,
 preferably one of
 the shorter and
 fatter shapes
pressed rose heads

selection of small
 silver metal shapes,
 such as stars
flat beads or buttons
tweezers

1 *Fill the saucepan with boiling water. Holding one end of the candle, dip the other end into the water for four to five seconds. Remove the candle from the water and immediately stick on as many of the pressed rose heads and decorations as you can before the wax hardens.*

2 *Repeat the process, turning the candle each time and not leaving it in the water for too long in case the wax melts around the decorated parts of the candle. A pair of tweezers may help to push the heavier items into the wax.*

Church candles are best for decorating, since they have a high proportion of beeswax and therefore burn for longer. They also soften and then harden more quickly than cheap paraffin wax candles.

Decorating
with Roses

The rose that lives its little hour

is prized beyond the sculptured flower.

William Cullen Bryant (1794–1832)

ROSE CROWNS

Roses can be enjoyed all year round. Garden roses start blooming in mid-spring and continue into late autumn if the weather is mild. During the barren winter months, there are still hundreds of commercially grown roses to choose from. Just as a garden enjoys a change of season with different colors, shapes and scents, you can acknowledge the shifting calendar inside your home. It is a practical investment to acquire a versatile container – perhaps an old china soup tureen or vase – that gives scope to a range of decorative ideas. It should be large enough to hold several small vases and candles, and also be deep enough to be used as a planter.

Right: A crown-shaped container is packed with an assortment of different shapes and sizes of jars and bottles. Fill these with water before arranging the flowers.

SPRING

Left: The darker pink and red freesias used in this arrangement have a stronger scent. Paler pink tulips present a contrast in shape to the 'Louise Odier' rose, a camellia-like Bourbon rose which flowers almost continuously through the summer. The delicate foliage of Bupleurum has the same lacy qualities as Alchemilla mollis, another good filler for later in the year.

SUMMER

Left: Sunflowers radiate bright vitality and are synonymous with hot summer days. The smaller-headed varieties are more practical for arrangements as those with heads the size of dinner plates are too heavy and dominating and are best left to grow in the garden. 'Tina' is one of the commercially grown, Larger-Flowered spray roses; it has a rich buttery color and a slight scent.

AUTUMN

Right: Rosa pimpinellifolia or 'Scotch Briar' is an ancient hardy rose which produces creamy-white single flowers and later almost black hips. The latter are combined here with the dusty pink and maroon mop heads of Hydrangea and a stunning commercially grown rose called 'Baccarole'. Its red wine-colored petals develop a faint but obvious perfume.

WINTER

Below: Create an elegant centerpiece for a Christmas table with white and cream roses, varying shades of green foliage and nondrip candles. Several very late-flowering 'Boule de Neige' Bourbon roses are supplemented with the commercially grown 'White Success'. Gray-green eucalyptus blends with Symphoricarpos (snowberry) and trailing variegated Hedera (common ivy).

STYLINGS FOR A DOZEN ROSES

The romantic tradition of giving a dozen red roses is all too often confined to Valentine's Day, when worldwide demand for red roses is so great that they become outrageously expensive. However, since roses are available all year round, why not use the idea of styling with a dozen roses for other times of the year?

Commercial rose breeders have at last recognized the universal desire for perfumed flowers and are producing exceptional roses that are scented. 'Prelude' is a beautiful dark lilac-colored rose that has a soft sweet perfume, which increases as the blooms open and can last for more than ten days.

Simple styling ideas

1 *Arrange the long-stemmed roses simply in a tall glass vase.*

2 *Buy or pick fresh green foliage to increase the size of your arrangement.*

3 *Using a rustic twig circle like the one on pages 62 and 63, tie small pieces of well-soaked florists' foam at intervals and cover them with foliage or moss. Carefully make small holes with a sharp stick in each piece. Place the roses in groups of two or three and keep the foam moist.*

4 *Make a table centerpiece of the roses in a basket with candles as on pages 46 and 47.*

5 *Line a large basket with polythene and fill with small compatible houseplants, leaving space for one or more vases to hold the roses. Cover the surface with moss to conceal the tops of the vases.*

6 *Before the roses open, hang them upside down to air-dry as on pages 40 and 41.*

7 *Once the roses have opened, but before they start to "blow," place them in a large shallow container of sand and allow to dry.*

Cut the roses to different lengths and mix with other flowers in several vases for more than one room.

Above: Combine the roses with complementary flowers such as darker pink arum lilies and lilac pink-streaked Alstroemeria (Peruvian lilies).

Above: Cut the roses very short and arrange in a bowl filled with a close-fitting piece of well-soaked florists' foam. Add pieces of foliage to create a rounded shape.

Right: Tie the roses into a pompom shape using a piece of string or garden raffia and place in a narrow glass vase or jam jar which is tall enough to support them. Stand this in a flowerpot or planter and cover the top with moss to create the effect of a tree. Keep well filled with water.

DRIED ROSE WREATH

Many flowers, including roses, dry beautifully and can be enjoyed for months after fresh flowers would have perished (see pages 40 and 41). Kept away from strong sunlight, which fades the petals, dried flowers need gentle dusting and a few drops of essential oils to keep them perfumed. As dried flowers are very fragile and easily broken, a wall-hanging wreath is an ideal way of arranging them and makes a country-style alternative to a picture.

1 Divide the rose buds into bunches of five and tie securely with the plant twists. Cut the stems of the rose buds to about 2 inches and use the ends of the plant twists to attach the bunches to the wreath. Do the same with the lavender bunches.

2 Tie the hydrangea heads to the ring of twigs so they conceal any stems and cover the twigs.

3 Attach the ribbon with a bow and loop it over a picture hook. Refresh with essential oil and dust carefully from time to time.

25 dried red rose buds

25 dried cream rose buds

paper-covered florists' wire

pruning shears or sharp scissors

a loosely woven ring of twigs

5 small bunches dried lavender

5 large dried hydrangea heads

red ribbon for hanging

A dried floral wreath will look wonderful hung on a wall. Combine with fresh flowers for special occasions.

ROSES IN DIFFERENT CONTAINERS

Virtually anything can be used to hold roses, from a simple jam jar to the most expensive crystal vase. What is more important is its shape – do try to avoid those types of vases with tight little necks that can take only a few stems, forcing them into an uncomfortable position. Allow the roses to be the centre of attention and increase their longevity by following the conditioning instructions on pages 38 and 39.

Left: A shallow glass bowl holding a couple of floating rose heads makes an effective small decoration for a bedside table or similar surface that is viewed from above. Shown here is the sweetly fragrant garden rose 'Iris Webb'.

Above: A few stems of roses make a stronger statement when held together with a piece of garden raffia. This rose is the commercially grown 'Prelude' with eucalyptus stems.

Left: Increase the impact of the blooms by grouping them in tumblers of contrasting jewel colours. The roses, left to right, are: 'Julia's Rose', 'Edith Holden', 'Iced Ginger', 'Peppermint Ice'. Front: 'Josephine Bruce'.

Right: The price of commercially grown roses is often determined by the stem length. Their straight stalks may be more than 24 inches long. This rose is commercially grown 'Konfetti'.

Below: If you regularly cut roses from the garden, a wide, shallow glass dish on a pedestal is a good choice for the irregularly shaped stems, particularly of old roses. Here is the garden rose 'Felicia'.

Right: A few sprays of a fragrant rose are all that are needed to impart scent to a small room or hallway. The picture shows the garden rose 'Amber Queen'. Cut roses from a bush carefully so as not to destroy the overall shape or strip it bare, choosing blooms that would otherwise be concealed from view.

TOPIARY ROSE TREE

This little double-headed tree makes a change from conventional arrangements. 'Yellow Dot' commercially grown spray roses open fully to a pretty rosette shape. The same design could be made up using dried rose buds, but you would need considerably more flowers and you would have to substitute dry foam spheres for the wet foam. Kept cool and frequently misted, this fresh rose tree should last for at least a week.

2 spheres and 1 rectangular block of florists' foam
sharp knife
pruning shears
sturdy terra-cotta pot
3 bamboo canes

thick pliable string
10 stems Leucadendron
10 stems spray roses
1 handful sphagnum moss

1 *Soak the florists' foam thoroughly. Cut a piece of the rectangular block to fit tightly into the pot. Insert the bamboo canes together and carefully position the foam spheres centrally on the canes. Bind the string around the canes and tie securely.*

2 *Cut off the Leucadendron heads, leaving about ³/₄ inch of stem, and insert into the foam spheres at regular intervals. Insert the roses in the same way. Cover the surface of the pot with the sphagnum moss to conceal the foam completely.*

For a really effective rose tree you need to select roses that open fully to provide a rosette shape. Remember to leave enough space around each rose for the bloom to open fully without being squashed.

'Yellow Dot' is a
commercially grown spray
rose that has numerous
rose heads on each stem.

$\mathscr{A}$ SINGLE ROSE

In the language of flowers, a single red rose signifies true love, and though this image may have been done to death, it is a powerful one, and a single perfect garden rose may still be picked and bestowed to good effect! Freshly cut from the garden and placed beside the bed of a guest or used as a centerpiece, a single rose may often be more stunning than a large arrangement of flowers. Any more than a single bloom of a heavily scented garden rose may also be too overpowering.

Below: This delightful rose, 'Edith Holden', was bred by an amateur rose grower in 1988. A turquoise green verdigris bowl filled with clear green glass pebbles and water scented with rose essential oil makes an effective decoration for a low table, a sideboard or beside a bed.

Above: Colored glass can emphasize the natural color of roses. The mauve pink color of this commercially grown and scented 'Prelude' rose is enhanced by the blue and green vase.

Above: Tiny liqueur or sherry glasses are perfect for a single stem or a small bunch of tiny roses like this 'Harmony Parade' Miniature rose.

Right: A collection of tiny glass bottles contains just one 'Shocking Blue' rose. Old perfume, oil and scent bottles are perfect vases for single stems and a row of such bottles makes an alternative arrangement to decorate a dining table. 'Shocking Blue' is a modern Cluster-Flowered rose that is actually lilac-colored rather than blue and has a delightful scent.

Right: 'Julia's Rose' is a Large-Flowered modern rose with an old-fashioned coppery pink shade. These subtly colored flowers are overtaking the more garishly colored roses produced in the 1950s and 1960s, and they blend more naturally with herbaceous borders filled with other soft-toned flowers. A small heavy-based glass vase supports the flower head.

Left: The 'Henri Matisse' rose is a new commercially grown rose and a great favorite among floral designers. It looks very similar to the oldest known striped Rosa gallica versicolor, or 'Rosa Mundi', first recorded in the twelfth century. Scattering rose petals across a dining table with the occasional bowl of scented floating candles and rose heads is an instant way of creating an elegant table setting.

69

A SIMPLE WEDDING BOUQUET

A simple bunch of freshly picked flowers is the most traditional form of flower arrangement and its natural beauty is the fashion for most modern brides. Rather than the tortured wiring of every stem, the flowers are arranged in the hand, creating a spiral effect by placing the stalks in one direction. This style of arrangement, known as the hand-tied or continental bouquet, is very popular in Europe, particularly in the Netherlands where it was first developed. Unlike the old-fashioned flat or sheaf bouquets where all the stems are of differing lengths, the hand-tied bouquet is ready to go straight into a vase without any further arranging. The linear hand-tied bouquet is a very romantic arrangement, perfect for brides with long flowing dresses. It may be held either pointing downwards or in the curve of an elbow. Yellow and white flowers are synonymous with spring and several branches of mimosa add a sharp, sweet fragrance to the bouquet.

5 stems mimosa
5 stems commercially grown spray roses 'Yellow Dot'
5 stems commercially grown spray roses 'Tina'
5 stems pale yellow tulips 'Montreux'
5 stems white tulips 'Casablanca'

5 stems white anemone
5 stems variegated pittosporum
5 stems trailing variegated ivy
string or raffia
sharp scissors
white or pale yellow ribbon

1 *Strip all the flowers and foliage leaves and thorns that would be below the binding point. As a rule of thumb this is about a third of the way up each stem. Thorns should be neatly cut off so as not to damage the rose stems. Place a rose, a stem of mimosa and one of pittosporum in one hand to form the bouquet's center.*

2 *With the other hand lay each subsequent stem at a 45-degree angle, always in the same direction. Turn the bouquet in the hand to gradually develop a spiral until complete. Hold the stems quite firmly at the binding point while adding in new flowers.*

3 *Twist the string or raffia just above the hand and then take it up and around the stems and tie. With sharp scissors trim all the stems to size, leaving a long slant at the end. Tie with ribbon.*

The bouquet needs to stand in water for as long as possible. Dry the stems before it is carried by the bride.

A HAND-TIED BOUQUET

This jewel-colored hand-tied bouquet is perfect for the less conventional bride or for those being married in winter who prefer bright tones. Make smaller versions for the bridesmaids.

Flowers have traditionally been used to symbolize emotions and the use of the floral language was very popular in Victorian times when specific flowers were worn as a discreet form of communication between the sexes. The language of flowers is still observed by some brides when they choose their bouquet and since the rose is associated with love, it is by far the most popular.

7 stems commercially
  grown rose 'First
  Red'
5 stems commercially
  grown rose
  'Ecstasy'
5 stems commercially
  grown rose
  'Leonardis'
5 stems commercially
  grown rose
  'Konfetti'

7 stems orange
  ranunculus
  ('Turban
  Buttercup')
5 stems viburnum
5 stems Liquidambar
  (sweet gum)
5 stems Cotinus
  (smoke bush)
sharp scissors
string or raffia
ribbon

THE LANGUAGE OF ROSES

Deep red rose	*Simplicity and beauty*	Red rose	*Eternal love*
Red rose buds	*Pure and lovely*	White rose	*Truth*
Single rose	*Simplicity*	White and red roses	*Unity*

1 *Prepare the ingredients by stripping off most of the rose leaves and all of those on the ranunculus and viburnum. Snip off all the rose thorns. Begin with a rose stem and lay a ranunculus stem over it.*

2 *Keeping the stems held upright, gradually add more stems to the bouquet at a 45-degree angle, turning the bouquet in your hand as you work to create the spiral effect.*

3 *Once you are satisfied with the overall size and shape of the bouquet, tie the stems together with raffia. Trim the stems neatly and finish off with a bright colored ribbon.*

Brightly-colored ribbon that matches the flowers or the dress covers the raffia or string. This bouquet is easily kept in water before it

is carried and may be made the day before the wedding to allow some of the flowers to start to open.

CORSAGES AND BUTTONHOLES

It used to be the fashion for gentlemen to present their ladies with an elaborate corsage of scented flowers to wear on a special occasion such as a grand ball. This custom is now restricted to wedding guests wearing rather boring carnations with a sprig of asparagus fern as buttonholes. With imagination and a little skill and expenditure, it is quite possible to create some really attractive arrangements to wear for formal occasions such as weddings or other special events. Traditional etiquette demands that ladies wear corsages with the flowers pointing downwards and gentlemen wear buttonholes with the flowers upright.

The finished buttonhole.

Gentleman's Buttonhole

1 stem commercially grown rose 'Ecstasy'
sharp scissors
medium-gauge florists' wire
gutta-percha tape
3 heads Eryngium (sea holly)
3 heads lavender
2 ivy leaves, wired as described in the steps
opposite for the Lady's Corsage

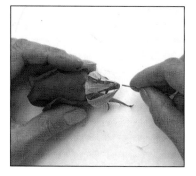

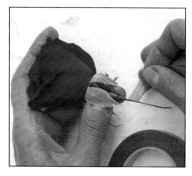

1 *Assemble all the ingredients. Cut the stem off the rose about ½ inch below the head. Push a small piece of medium-gauge florists' wire through the remaining stem up into the head. Check that the wire feels quite secure and not likely to become loose.*

2 *The gutta-percha tape is rubber-based and seals under pressure. Pull the tape so it stretches and bind it around the stem and wire, sealing them together. Repeat this step around the Eryngium stems and the lavender to create two little bunches.*

3 *Wire the ivy leaves (see opposite page). Then arrange one individual flower with the ivy leaves so that the leaves form a flat back to the buttonhole. Ensure that the ends are completely covered.*

4 *To make the ivy leaves more stable, create a "loop" of wire to support each leaf.*

Lady's Corsage

medium-gauge florists' wire
2 stems commercially grown roses 'First Red'
fine rose wire
2 large and 1 smaller ivy leaves
florists' adhesive tape
sharp scissors
2 sprigs Cotoneaster berries
coordinating ribbon, preferably wired

The finished corsage.

1 Wire the roses as described opposite. Thread the fine wire through the main vein at the back of each ivy leaf. Leave a long end of wire at one end.

2 Take the shorter wire over the stem, around the back and down. Wind the longer wire round both stem and other wire and tape.

3 Group the roses and berries together, using the ivy leaves as the flat back, and bind the stems together. Finish with a ribbon.

Present buttonholes and corsages in tiny boxes protected by colored tissue paper to help keep them fresh until they are worn.

Bathtime & Boudoir

Then will I raise aloft the milk-white rose,

For whose sweet smell the air shall be perfumed.

WILLIAM SHAKESPEARE (1564–1616)

AROMATHERAPHY

Cave paintings found in France show that flowers and plants were used therapeutically as long ago as 1000 BC. The Ancient Egyptians discovered methods of extracting the oils from plants to make perfumes, flavor food, produce salves and ointments and, importantly, to embalm the dead. These skills and recipes spread across the world to the civilizations of Ancient Greece, India and China, eventually emerging in Europe.

The term aromatherapy – the treatment of ailments with essential oils – was first used by the French chemist Gattefosse, who researched their medicinal properties in the 1920s. Essential oils are the concentrated essences obtained from flowers, leaves, berries and bark by various means of extraction.

Rose essential oil is one of the most expensive and is often sold mixed with a small amount of carrier oil such as jojoba. Each essential oil has different qualities and values that a qualified aromatherapist can use to create a program of holistic treatment.

Massage is one of the most effective methods of experiencing the healing properties of these oils. You can create your own massage oil, but it is best to make only a small quantity at a time and keep it in a dark glass bottle with the lid screwed on tightly. Never apply straight essential oil directly to the skin unless under the supervision of a qualified aromatherapist. Though recommended in many books, it is also unwise to add straight essential oils to a bath, since the oil may appear to disperse but will not actually do so and can therefore come in direct contact with the skin causing an allergic reaction. Essential oils can be immensely beneficial but need to be used with care.

1 *Mix several essential oils together in a base of carrier oil such as grapeseed, jojoba or sweet almond to produce a massage oil that has specific therapeutic benefits.*

2 *Never exceed 1 drop of essential oil for every 20 drops of carrier oil. These oils should be purchased in dropper bottles so it is easy to be accurate when making up your own blends.*

Aphrodisiac Massage Oil

A light, nongreasy and fragrant oil for a sensual massage over the entire body that is relaxing and luxurious.

5 drops rose essential oil
3 drops ylang-ylang essential oil
2 drops jasmine essential oil
7 tbsp grapeseed oil
1 tsp wheat-germ oil

Harmonious Massage Oil

These essential oils combined create a harmony related to the ability to love and be loved. Rose has healing and sensual qualities; sandalwood is relaxing and sensual; sage, euphoric and uplifting; geranium, cleansing and refreshing; ginger, fortifying and warming.

13 drops rose essential oil
2 drops sandalwood essential oil
2 drops sage essential oil
3 drops geranium essential oil
3 drops ginger essential oil
4 tsp jojoba oil
7 tbsp unrefined sunflower oil

Rose essential oil is one of the most precious and luxurious of all perfumed flower oils.

After-Sun Soothing Oil

Sunbathing, particularly in the middle and hottest part of the day, can have a devastating effect on the skin. It encourages premature aging and can be very painful. Prevention is, of course, better than cure, but if you are feeling tender, and providing the skin is not actually burnt and broken, this massage oil can be very comforting and moisturizing.

5 drops rose essential oil
5 drops chamomile essential oil
3 tbsp grapeseed oil
3 tbsp virgin olive oil
1 tbsp wheat-germ oil

BATH BODY CARE

The emperor Nero is said to have bathed in pure rose water and extended this luxury to guests at his frequent banquets, probably contributing to the economic collapse of the Roman Empire! The following simple beauty formulas won't break the bank but are easy to concoct and when presented in pretty bottles make lovely gifts.

Rose Body Lotion

2 tbsp water, boiled
¼ tsp borax
1 tsp white beeswax
1 tsp lanolin
2 tbsp petroleum jelly
5 tsp apricot kernel oil
4 tsp cold-pressed sunflower oil
10 drops rose essential oil
1 drop pink food coloring

Dissolve the borax in the boiled water. Melt the beeswax, lanolin and petroleum jelly with the apricot kernel and cold-pressed sunflower oils in a double boiler. Remove from the heat once the wax has melted and stir well. Add the borax solution whisking as you do so. The lotion will quickly turn white and thicken, but keep whisking until cool. Then add the rose oil and food coloring. Pour the lotion into a tinted glass jar and store in a cool place.

Rose-scented Seashells, Pebbles and Pumice

Collect small seashells and pebbles polished smooth from the effect of waves.

Mix them together in a decorative bowl. Add a few drops of rose-scented room scent or oil. The slightly porous surfaces will absorb the perfume and create a soft aroma in a room.

Tiny pumice stones available from chemists or specialist shell shops are particularly good for soaking up scent.

Use only a few drops of the essential oil at a time to create a pleasing aroma.

Body lotion scented with rose essential oil is luxuriously relaxing and soothing on the skin.

The wonderfully uplifting nature of rose scent makes it the perfect accompaniment to any bathtime treat.

Luxurious Body Scrub

This is a delightful alternative to the loofah, much more gentle and pleasantly aromatic. Simply mix all the ingredients in a bowl before you require it. After a bath dry yourself thoroughly and rub the mixture into your skin, paying particular attention to dry areas. Let it dry on the skin and then rub off using a soft wash cloth.

1 tbsp powdered orange rind
3 tbsp ground almonds
1 tbsp oatmeal
approximately 6 tbsp almond oil
5 drops essential rose oil

FACIAL BEAUTY

The most delicate skin on the body's surface is on the face, and though true beauty comes from within, there is nothing quite so attractive as a fresh and clear face that vibrates with good health. Millions are spent each year on beautifying lotions, particularly those reputed to forestall the onset of aging. Rose essential oil is nourishing and moisturizing and three to four drops mixed with 4 tsp jojoba oil makes a simple but effective facial oil to apply after the skin has been thoroughly cleansed.

Rose Cream Cleanser and Face Masks

7 tbsp triple-distilled rose water
3 tbsp heavy cream
2 tbsp pure unblended clear honey
2 tbsp fine ground oatmeal

This simple cleanser is mildly astringent with both soothing and cooling properties. It should be made in small quantities and kept in the refrigerator. If you reduce the rose water to 1 tbsp and replace it with the honey that has been gently warmed, you have a face mask suitable for dry skin but gentle enough for sensitive faces. Adding the oatmeal, stirring well and

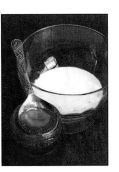

Mix the rose water with the cream and stir well. Keep in an airtight container in a cool place.

This honey, cream and rose water facial mask should be smoothed over the face and neck.

Above: The addition of oatmeal makes an exfoliating face mask which should be gently rinsed off after ten minutes.

Opposite: 'Awakening' is a climbing rose with fully double blooms that flower continually through the summer.

letting sit for ten minutes produces a mask that can also be used as an exfoliating skin scrub. As with all face masks, this is most effective if used while relaxing in a bath and left on the face and neck for about ten minutes before washing off very thoroughly.

Rose and Chamomile Facial Steam

Hot water facials open the skin's pores and not only make the face feel refreshed and thoroughly clean, but also create a woderful sense of well-being and general relaxation. Fill a bowl that is just wider than your face with hot water and then add three drops of rose essential oil and four drops chamomile essential oil. Cover your head with a towel and drape it over the bowl.

Five minutes is usually long enough to feel the benefit. If possible, relax somewhere quiet and dark with subdued lighting for another 15 minutes before applying one of the following toning lotions.

For dry skin, mix 5 tbsp triple-distilled rose water with 2 tbsp orange flower water; for oily skin, 6 tbsp triple-distilled rose water with 2 tbsp witch hazel. Combine the ingredients in scrupulously clean bottles and keep cool.

HANDS AND NAILS

To keep hands and nails looking their best, regular use of a good hand cream and a weekly manicure makes a noticeable difference. For the two hand oils listed below, mix the ingredients together and store in dark-colored bottles when not in use.

Rose Hand Oil

¼ cup jojoba oil
¼ cup almond oil
6 drops rose essential oil
4 drops sandalwood essential oil

Massaging the hands daily keeps the fingers and palms soft and smooth, and the combination of these essential oils is particularly suited to drier and more mature skins. Make sure you massage the backs of the hands to protect against the damaging effects of the sun, which can cause liver spots.

Rose Nail Oil

¼ cup almond oil
2tsp apricot kernel oil
5 drops geranium essential oil
2 drops rose essential oil

Massaging the base of your nails every day will encourage healthy growth. You can also use this oil as part of a manicure, soaking the nails for at least ten minutes after you have thoroughly cleaned them.

Rose Hand Cream

This fragrant hand cream is rich in nourishing oils and waxes. Two bowls of thin clear liquids when combined miraculously produce a thick white mixture that has the consistency of cream cheese.

¼ cup rose water
3 tbsp witch hazel
½ tsp glycerine
¼ tsp borax
2 tbsp emulsifying wax or white beeswax
1 tsp lanolin
2 tbsp almond oil
2 drops rose essential oil

MAKING HAND CREAM

1 *Gently heat the rose water, witch hazel, glycerine and borax in a saucepan until the borax has dissolved. In a double-boiler melt the wax, lanolin and almond oil over a gentle heat.*

2 *Slowly add the rose water mixture to the oil mixture, stirring constantly as you do so. It will quickly turn milky and thicken. Remove from the heat and continue to stir while it cools and then add the rose essential oil. Pour the cream into china or glass jars and store in a cool place.*

'Madame Alfred Carrière' is a sweet-smelling climbing rose, which, unusually, can survive being grown on north-facing walls.

THE PERFUME OF ROSES

The discovery of rose oil, or attar of roses as it is also known, is generally attributed to Avicenna, a tenth-century Arab physician. However, from clay tablets found in tombs dated around 1500 BC, it is known that the Ancient Egyptians used perfumed oils for both anointing the living and embalming the dead. The rose has quite the most feminine and seductive perfume of all the essential oils. Women clearly recognized the aphrodisiac quality of the rose as well as jasmine and musk. Madame de Pompadour, the mistress of Louis XV of France, attached very small scented stars and crescents to intimate parts of her body to delight the King as he searched for them. Much earlier, Cleopatra drenched the sails of her royal barge with perfume before she sailed to encounter Mark Antony for the first time. Conversely, Victorian ladies were so wary of the sexual powers of perfume that they opted for carrying scented handkerchiefs rather than take the dire risk of wearing it directly on their bodies.

Pure attar of roses is a highly concentrated oil and perfume and it takes about two tons of rose petals of the same fragrance to produce just 2¼ lb of essential oil. Rose otto, which is the name of the essential oil, is made from the petals of *Rosa damascena*, grown in Morocco

'Crown Rose' was reputedly the favorite perfume of Alexandra, wife of Edward VII.

and Turkey, and on the Balkan foothills in Bulgaria. Like other very expensive essential oils such as jasmine and neroli (bitter orange), it is often sold in a dilution comprising 10 percent rose oil and 90 percent jojoba oil. This combination not only makes a rich and sensual perfume but is also recommended for skin problems from eczema to wrinkles, general

puffiness and congestion of the pores.

Rose absolute is produced from the pink *R. centifolia* and these roses have been cultivated by French perfumers in Grasse for hundreds of years. Though many modern scents contain chemicals that recreate natural fragrances, the better quality, more expensive perfumes include pure rose oil as one of their constituents. Chanel No. 5 is undoubtedly one of the most famous; other classics include Joy from Patou, Guy Laroche's Fidji and the more contemporary Rive Gauche from Yves Saint Laurent. The Crown Perfumery Company was established in London in 1872 and relaunched in 1994. The following year it reintroduced Crown Rose, reputedly the favorite perfume of Queen Alexandra, wife of Edward VII.

The fragrance of roses may also be enjoyed as an air freshener by adding a few drops to the water in a spray gun and spritzing the atmosphere. Spraying also has the effect of lowering a room's temperature by displacing heat particles. Those decadent Romans cooled off their guests by spraying them with rose water. It is also a lovely way to refresh and cleanse the face after a long, hard day.

With yellow and pink shading, these apricot roses are the scented blooms of the modern Climber 'Compassion'.

Rose Gifts

It is at the edge of the petal

that love waits.

WILLIAM CARLOS WILLIAMS (1883–1963)

ROSE BOUQUETS

Simple, hand-tied bouquets are a special gift, and their diminutive size implies an intimacy that makes them personal and unique. If the flowers are home-grown, they will be all the more appreciated by the recipient. The smaller the bouquet, the tinier and more delicate the flowers and foliage need to be. Wispy, frond-like leaves define the shape of individual flower heads, particularly if the colors are similar, and this gives the bouquet more clarity.

Before arranging the flowers make sure that all the lower leaves have been removed, including rose thorns, which should be cut off neatly with scissors. The spherical shape is achieved by spiraling the stems, as shown on pages 70 to 73, and the perfect hand-tied bouquet should be able to stand on its stems. Practice is essential if you are to perfect this technique and it is far easier to start with small

bouquets before progressing to larger ones. An outer layer of firm leaves also shields the flowers and is far more natural than the old-fashioned foil or paper collars.

If the bouquet has to be transported or you want to make more of the gift, an old shoe box covered in wrapping paper both protects the flowers and offers an element of surprise. Wrapping a little moistened tissue around the stem ends will keep the flowers fresh for several hours.

Whether the bouquet is of fresh or dried flowers, wrapping the stems in ribbon makes it easier to carry, especially for weddings.

Left: Present your bouquet in a decorative box.
Right: The roses used in the bouquets, clockwise from top left are: 'Boule de Neige', 'Purple Prince', 'Blush Noisette' and 'Baccarole'.

1 Bind the flowers with raffia and trim the stems. Leaving enough ribbon to tie a bow, start winding the ribbon from the top overlapping each twist to conceal the raffia and the stems.

2 When you reach the bottom, tuck the ribbon over the base of the stems and then wind the ribbon back up the stems.

3 When you reach the starting point, tie the ribbon in a knot before adding a bow and cut the ribbon ends on a slant to help to prevent any fraying.

ROSE-SCENTED TEA AND SUGAR

Scented teas and sugars are simplicity itself, but presented in decorative containers they are an original gift idea for tea-lovers and cooks. Extravagantly wrapped with a box of the Festival Shortbreads or Rose-water Cookies on pages 114 and 115, they make presents for special festive occasions.

Rose-scented Tea

The rose petals in this beverage subtly flavor and add a distinctive scent to a high-quality tea such as oolong. This tea, named from the Chinese words *wu* (black), and *lung* (dragon), combine the qualities of black and green teas.

The finest blends, known as Formosa oolongs, come from Taiwan and have a rich amber color and a delicious fruity taste. Pouchong teas are mixed with jasmine and gardenia flowers, and you can make your own special blend with rose petals.

7 oz highly scented dried rose petals
1¼ lb finest quality tea

Mix together well in a large bowl and divide among airtight containers, preferably pretty screw-top jars or decorative tea caddies. Use as any other fine quality tea.

Rose-scented Sugar

This delicate sugar has a multitude of uses. It can be used to sweeten cakes and sauces, stirred into cream or yogurt for a subtle flavoring and substituted for the sugar used in the Rose-water Cookies on page 114.

5 cups highly scented dried rose petals
1 cup sugar

Grind the rose petals in a food processor until they are the consistency of coarse sand, but not a powder. You can use a coffee grinder, but first make sure all traces of coffee have been wiped off, or its strong flavor will obliterate the rose fragrance.

Mix the petals with the sugar and transfer into screw-top jars. Make sure you use only the finest-quality rose petals that have been thoroughly dried.

Left: Careful thought taken on the presentation of your gifts, even if they are simple cookies, will make all the difference to the recipient.

Right: Loose tea scented with petals and rose heads and rose-scented sugar make fine gifts for a special treat.

CHOCOLATES AND CANDIES

For special occasions such as birthdays and at Christmas, handmade chocolates and candies make a delightfully indulgent gift. Use decorative boxes or tins to contain the treats.

Swedish Rose Chocolate Balls

This is a very rich chocolate sweet that could be easily made by children if the rum were omitted. It is made by my Swedish friend Kent Turnefelt as a Christmas treat.

5 oz good-quality dessert chocolate
2 tbsp ground almonds
2 tbsp sugar
2 large egg yolks
2 tsp strong coffee or coffee extract
1 tbsp dark rum
1 tbsp triple-distilled rose water
¼ cup chocolate vermicelli

Grind the chocolate and add to all the other ingredients except the rose water and vermicelli. Make into tiny balls by rolling small teaspoonfuls between your fingers. Chill well. Dip into the rose water and roll in the chocolate vermicelli.

Tie up the chocolate balls in a circle of clear plastic wrap with tiny pieces of natural raffia.

Rose Petal Truffles

An indulgent treat that demands the finest-quality chocolate with at least 60 percent cocoa solids. You may replace the rose water with brandy if you prefer a less sweet flavor.

1¼ lb semisweet chocolate
1¼ cups heavy cream
1tbsp triple-distilled rose water
2 drops rose essential oil
9 oz semisweet chocolate for coating
candied rose petals

Melt the chocolate and cream together in a double-boiler until completely combined and soft in texture. Add the rose water and essential oil. Pour the mixture into a baking tin lined with nonstick or waxed paper. Leave to cool and when the mixture is nearly firm, take teaspoonfuls of the chocolate and shape into balls in your hands. Chill the truffles until they are quite hard.

Melt the chocolate for coating the truffles in the double boiler. Skewer a truffle and dip it into the melted chocolate, making sure it is completely covered. Leave the finished truffles on a sheet of nonstick or waxed paper to cool, placing a candied rose petal on each one before the chocolate sets.

Keep these truffles in the refrigerator.

Rose Turkish Delight

In the Middle East, these sweets are served with tiny cups of very strong coffee.

4 tbsp triple-distilled rose water
2 tbsp powdered gelatin
1¾ cups granulated sugar
⅔ cup water
red coloring
9 drops rose essential oil
¼ cup roughly chopped
blanched almonds
¼ cup cornstarch
⅓ cup confectioners' sugar

Pour the rose water into a bowl and sprinkle with the gelatin. Dissolve the granulated sugar in the water in a saucepan over a low heat. When the syrup is clear, boil until it reaches 234°F on a sugar thermometer. Remove from the heat and add the gelatin and rose water. Return to a low heat, stirring, until the gelatin has dissolved. Remove from the heat, and add a few drops of red coloring. Add the rose oil and almonds and pour the syrupy mixture into a 6–7 inch oiled baking pan and set aside. When set, cut into pieces. Sift the cornstarch and confectioners' sugar together and sprinkle onto the cut pieces.

Spear the Turkish delights with orange sticks to keep the confectioners' sugar mixture from covering your hands.

ROSE WRAPPING, CARDS AND GIFT TAGS

The presentation of a gift adds the finishing touch, which can transform a very simple and modest item into something extravagant and exciting. The careful selection of paper and trimmings shows just how much thought and time have been taken for the recipient and these sentiments are always appreciated. Even the most basic brown paper may be sprayed with an alcohol-based perfume – essential oils tend to stain – and the package tied with garden raffia made into an exuberant bow securing a small bunch of rose buds.

Some gifts are difficult to wrap. They are unwieldy shapes or so obvious in shape that a disguise is needed to keep the recipient guessing. Collect containers such as shoe boxes, which can be covered with gift wrap and padded with layers of tissue.

Decorative rubber stamps dipped in colorful inks change plain papers into decorated wrapping and the soft ribbons found on haberdashery counters are much more luxurious than those sold in stationery shops. Tiny gold and silver metallic stars can be stuck to plain papers for a glittery effect and also sprinkled inside the wrapping to create an unexpected shower as the present is opened.

Gift Tags

1 *To press petals and leaves, place the flower heads or petals facedown on blotting paper and cover the area with plant material of a similar thickness, taking care not to squash the flowers or overlap them. Cover with blotting paper and press for several weeks. If you do not have a flower press, then several heavy books will work just as well.*

2 *After several weeks the flowers and leaves should be completely dry, wafer-thin and very fragile. Don't be surprised if some of the original colors have either darkened or faded.*

3 *Using a paper glue, carefully stick the flowers and leaves in a design on colored cardboard or, for a layered effect, use a paler or white inset paper. Handmade, rough textured papers are particularly suitable. To create a "torn" edge, wet the paper until it is moist but not soaked and gently tear the shape you require.*

4 *Punch a hole in the card and thread a piece of raffia or fine string for tying to the packet.*

Christmas Gift Box

1 Cover a box with plain white paper. Using multipurpose glue, squeeze dots over the top and sides and scatter metallic stars and crescents. Shake off the loose shapes and save.

2 Cut a piece of contrasting ribbon to the right length and tie around the box, knotting it in the center of the lid.

3 Attach a tiny bouquet of roses to the knot with more of the same ribbon. Finish by tying the remainder of the ribbon into a bow.

Homemade cards and wrapping make gifts more personal and a pleasure to receive.

MINIATURE ROSES

A long-lasting gift for rose-lovers is *Rosa chinensis*, the pygmy or China rose. These Miniature varieties are commercially bred in Europe from the species that originated from China. As they are available in flower year-round, they make a delightful alternative to cut flowers. Of the new varieties, 'Parade' stays in flower longer than other types and is grown in a range of colors: 'Royal Parade' (mid pink), 'Fashion Parade' (pale pink), 'Victory Parade' (red), 'Dreaming Parade' (salmon pink) and 'Harmony Parade' (pale peach pink).

These plants prefer constantly moist soil and good humidity. Once they have flowered, they can be planted outside in the garden or in pots on a patio. Too dry an atmosphere causes immature buds to drop off and a vigilant check of the plants is needed, since they are susceptible to red spider mites and aphids. Good air circulation usually prevents this problem.

After this miniature rose is planted in the garden, it will cease to maintain its tiny form and may grow to about 12 inches. Cuttings may be taken in the spring, dipping each one in hormone-rooting powder before planting in a good-quality potting compost.

basket
polythene
scissors
adhesive tape
crocks

compost
3 *miniature rose*
plants
moss

Other flowers and foliage that combine well with these tiny rose heads need to be of a similar proportion such as Narcissi, lily-of-the-valley, lavender, Nepeta mussinii, Campanula or Viola plants.

1 *Line the basket with polythene, securing it with adhesive tape.*

2 *Arrange crocks over the base of the basket. Fill with compost.*

3 *Remove the rose plants from their pots and place in the basket.*

4 *Pack moss into any spaces and cover the soil.*

Above: Three Miniature roses planted in a long basket interspersed with herbs such as oregano, thyme or bush basil make an inside window-box for a kitchen or bathroom.

Above: Another idea is to make a fragrant pot au fleur using a basket that will hold a couple of Miniature roses and a small vase of highly scented flowers.

PAPER AND SILK ROSES

Artificial flowers, especially roses, can look horrendous. There is nothing more off-putting than a window display consisting of a dusty arrangement of gaudy-colored, plastic blooms, particularly if the shop happens to be a florist. There are, however, some extremely striking silk or taffeta roses in gentle, muted colors that would be perfect for evening dresses or on extravagant hats.

Long-lasting and resilient barettes made with fabric roses are ideal for bridesmaids who cannot resist putting their hands in their hair every few minutes, so you can keep the fresh flowers for bouquets or small baskets. One or two large cabbage-style paper roses transform a simple straw hat into a sophisticated creation

White silk roses add a splash of color in winter to this foliage houseplant.

fit for the most elegant wedding or garden party. While artificial roses can never take the place of the real thing, both high-quality silk and paper roses are appropriate and long-lasting for hair and hat decorations, and it is worth seeking the best imitations around.

Rose Barette

This technique may be used to glue fabric roses onto scrunchies, hair bands or hat ribbons.

glue gun with multipurpose glue sticks
metal barette
fabric roses with leaves

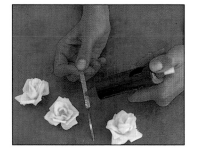

1 *Always take great care with glue guns, since the glue is very hot. Insert the glue stick and wait for the gun to heat up. The trigger will pull when glue has turned to liquid.*

2 *Squeeze an even line of glue along the top edge of the barette, always keeping your fingers well clear of the piping hot glue.*

3 *Stick the rose heads to the slide pointing to alternate sides, so that their bases are completely covered.*

4 *Reverse the slide and add more glue to stick fabric leaves to the slide to fill any remaining gaps.*

Beautiful imitation paper roses.

The Edible Rose

They that have roses
Never need bread.

Dorothy Parker (1893–1967)

CELEBRATION ROSE AND FRUIT CAKE

This deliciously rich fruit cake is perfect for celebrations such as birthdays or christenings. Covered with a delicately flavored rose water icing, it is decorated with whole edible candied rose blooms.

Rose and Fruit Cake

MAKES ONE 8-IN ROUND OR 7-IN
SQUARE CAKE

1 cup golden raisins

2¼ cups currants

1 cup raisins

1 tbsp brandy or very strong
rose-hip tea

2 cups all-purpose flour

1½ tsp pumpkin-pie spice

½ tsp ground nutmeg

½ tsp ground cinnamon

generous pinch of salt

¾ cup butter or margarine

¾ cup soft dark brown sugar

½ tsp grated orange zest

3 large eggs

⅓ cup candied cherries

¼ cup candied orange peel

⅓ cup chopped almonds

1 tbsp black molasses

Oven temperature: 275°F

Mix the dried fruits together with the brandy or rose-hip tea in a large bowl, then cover and let it marinate overnight. Grease and line the base and sides of a 8-inch round or 7-inch square cake pan.

Sift together the flour, spices and salt in a large bowl. In a separate bowl, beat the butter or margarine, sugar and orange zest together until light and creamy. Add 1 tbsp of the flour mixture before adding each of the eggs to the butter mixture. Fold in the remaining flour mixture and stir in the marinated fruit, candied cherries, candied peel, almonds and molasses.

Spoon the mixture into the prepared pan and level the surface. Cover the top with a double layer of waxed paper with a 1-inch diameter air-hole cut in the center. Tie a double layer of waxed paper around the outside of the pan, so it stands at least 2 inch above the rim. This is important, since it prevents the cake from burning. Bake the cake on the lowest shelf for four and a half hours; do not open the door while it is cooking. Let the cake cool completely before icing.

Fondant Rose Icing

5½ cups confectioners' sugar

2 egg whites

1 tsp triple-distilled rose water

½ tsp lemon juice

½ cup liquid glucose

Stir the confectioners' sugar into a bowl and beat in the egg whites, rose water, lemon juice and liquid glucose with a wooden spoon. Knead until the mixture forms a firm dough.

1 *Spread the cake top and sides with rose jelly to encourage the icing to stick. Roll out the icing on a cool surface dusted with confectioners' sugar.*

2 *Rub the surface of the icing with confectioners' sugar for an even covering. Use the rolling pin to position the icing over the cake. Cut off any excess.*

Fresh blooms of 'Nimbus' and 'Shocking Blue' roses decorate the table.

CANDIED ROSE PETALS

It is essential, of course, that the rose petals used for any of these recipes are collected from bushes that have not been sprayed with any sort of pesticide and are not grown near a busy road. Pick fresh full blooms carefully, rinse and dry the petals thoroughly, and then remove the white triangle at the base of each petal. When candying complete blooms, leave a short piece of stem to hold them by.

1 *Each petal or bloom must be completely covered with a thin, even layer of lightly beaten egg white. Use a paintbrush that gets into the cracks and crevices and do not forget the undersides of the petals. Any uncoated parts will turn brown and shrivel up. The process must be done quickly before the egg white dries. After the third or fourth rose you will get the knack.*

2 *Sprinkle sifted confectioners' sugar over evenly and shake off the excess, otherwise any blobs will cause a patchy effect. This may be desirable to create light and shade contrast, but a regular, even coating will preserve the roses more successfully.*

3 *Allow petals or blooms to dry on a wire rack. Stored between layers of tissue paper, the petals will keep for about a week. Do not put sugar petals in the refrigerator or they will "weep" – keep in a dry and cool place.*

Candied rose heads and petals are a delicious way to decorate cakes and desserts.

ROSE TEA

In summer, when garden roses are in glorious abundance, you can use the fragrant petals to make rose jelly to spread on scones with lashings of thick crème fraîche. Less indulgent are some delicious rose-petal sandwiches.

Rose Jelly

This pretty pink jelly may be used to sweeten yogurts or cottage cheese and as a condiment with cold roasted chicken and to flavor light meat sauces.

MAKES 1¼ LB

1¼ lb sugar

3⅔ cups water

11 oz scented rose petals

¾ cup lemon juice

5 tbsp commercial pectin

5 tbsp rose water

Dissolve the sugar in the water with the petals and lemon juice by heating gently in a large saucepan. Bring to a boil and simmer for about 30 minutes. Pour into a large nylon sieve lined with cheesecloth, and leave to drip through overnight.

Add the pectin and rose water to the liquid and bring to a boil until setting point is

Above: Heart-shaped rose-petal sandwiches.

Opposite: A complete rose tea decorated with 'Black Tea', 'Shocking Blue' and pale pink miniature roses.

reached (220°F on a sugar thermometer). Remove from the heat, decant into warmed, sterilized jars. Cover with waxed paper circles and seal. When cold, label and date them.

Rose Petal Sandwiches

These dainty sandwiches make a healthier alternative to cake or biscuits and may be served with a refreshing cup of rose-scented tea or a rose-hip tisane.

SERVES 8

1 cup unsalted butter

5 heads scented roses, either dark pink or red

1 loaf soft, thinly sliced bread

Cut the block of butter in half lengthwise and place each half on a dish lined with a thick layer of rose petals. Cover the sides and top of the butter generously with more petals. Cover with a lid or layer of cheesecloth and let sit for 24 hours in the refrigerator.

Discard the top layer of petals and allow the butter to soften slightly before spreading onto very thin slices of bread. Use a heart-shaped pastry cutter to cut out the center of each slice and add a thin layer of fresh rose petals before putting the slices together to make sandwiches.

ROSE WINES AND PUNCHES

There is a freshness and intensity of flavor in homemade wines and punches that is very rarely present in commercial counterparts. It is also fun making your own drinks to serve to guests on a hot summer's day. The extra effort you have put into your al fresco party will not go unnoticed. These recipes are meant to be drunk the day they're made – keep them cool in the refrigerator until serving.

The pendulous hips in the center are R. moyesii, which have pinky-red single flowers; the black hips are R. pimpinellifolia, a very ancient Scottish rose bearing masses of creamy white flowers; the hips in the trug on the left are 'Frau Dagmar Hartopp', a rose pink single-bloom flower, which grows on a very fresh green compact bush bearing crimson hips; the hips on the right are 'Hansa' rose, which are large and full with a red-violet color; the hips in the bucket are 'Scabrosa', another of the rugosa species, with velvet crimson-mauve single blooms and fat, rich hips.

Rose-hip Wine

Traditionally, hedgerow rose hips were gathered to make wine but if you do not live in the country, you could grow a hedge of *Rosa rugosa*, one of the few wild roses that produces exceptionally large, round hips.

MAKES ABOUT 6 BOTTLES
9 cups rose hips
8 pints boiling water
3½ cups granulated sugar
juice of 1 lemon and 1 orange
½ oz fresh baker's yeast

Coarsely mince the rose hips in a food processor, put into a plastic bucket and cover with boiling water. Stir with a long-handled wooden spoon. Let stand for three days, stirring daily. Strain through a cheesecloth.

Make a syrup by heating the sugar with the fruit juices. Add the syrup to the rose-hip juice and pour into a fermentation jar. Cream the yeast with a little of the liquid, set aside to ferment, then add to the wine. Add more boiled, cooled water to bring the liquid to within 1 inch of the top of the jar. Fit an airlock and leave in a warm place to ferment. Decant into a clean jar, let sit for another three months and then bottle.

Right: The roses here are the Modern Shrub 'Felicia'.

Rose Petal Punch

Fragrant rose petals can be used both to flavor and decorate modest sparkling wines to create a celebratory punch, perfect for a party on a summer's day.

SERVES 8
11 oz scented rose petals
⅓ cup sugar
7 tbsp framboise (raspberry liqueur)
1 bottle dry white wine, chilled
1 bottle demi-sec sparkling wine or champagne, chilled
extra petals or blooms to decorate

1 *In a large bowl, sprinkle the petals with sugar, pour over the framboise. Cover and chill for an hour. Add the wine and chill for another hour.*

2 *Pour through a sieve into a glass jug. Add the sparkling wine or champagne. Decorate with rose petals or full blooms just before you serve it.*

ROSE CORDIAL, JAM AND VINEGAR

To make the most of the wonderful array of rose petals in the summer months, here are recipes for a delicious cordial, a tasty jam and an unusual salad vinegar, all designed to enhance your guests' table.

Rose Petal Cordial

A light refreshing drink to serve in early summer or when roses are in abundance.

SERVES 8

25 heads scented roses, including extra petals
for decoration
4 cups granulated sugar
3½ pints boiled or bottled
still water, cold
½ lemon, preferably unwaxed, sliced
sparkling mineral water

Remove the rose petals carefully from the heads and put into a large pan or bowl with the sugar, water and sliced lemon. Stir three or four times during a 24-hour period. Strain and decant into clean glass bottles. Dilute to taste with the mineral water, adding fresh rose petals for decoration.

Right: The rose here is 'Amber Queen'.

Rose Petal Jam

A delicate preserve for scones with cream.

MAKES 1½ LB

6 cups granulated sugar
3⅔ cups water
5 oz scented rose petals
¾ cup lemon juice
5 tbsp commercial pectin
3 tbsp rose water

Dissolve the sugar in the water with the petals and lemon juice by heating gently in a large saucepan. Bring to a boil and simmer for about 30 minutes. Add the pectin and rose water and stir together. Boil rapidly for five minutes. Test for setting point (220°F), using a sugar thermometer. Alternatively, put a teaspoonful of jam on a cold saucer and put in the refrigerator for about five minutes. Then tilt the saucer and if the jam does not run, it is ready for canning. It is a good idea to test every few minutes to avoid overboiling.

Cool the jam for ten minutes, and then pour carefully into warm, sterilized jars. Cover with waxed paper circles and seal. When the jars are completely cold, label and date the jam.

Rose Petal Vinegar

This vinegar may be used in a dressing for summer salads and it is also effective as a cool compress to ease a nagging headache.

MAKES 1¼ CUPS
1¼ cups good quality white
wine vinegar
scented red rose petals

1 *Pull the rose petals from the flower heads. Scald the vinegar by bringing it to just below boiling point and allow to cool.*

2 *Snip off any blemished part of the petals. Prepare enough petals to fill a cup and put into a large glass jar or bottle.*

3 *Add the cooled vinegar, cover very tightly with screw-top or cork and leave on a sunny windowsill for at least three weeks.*

Right: Rose Petal Vinegar.

ROSE HONEY AND SHORTBREAD

Rose water is a delightful and adaptable ingredient to add to cakes and cookies to give them that subtle taste of summer.

Rose Petal Honey

This aromatic honey makes an inexpensive and thoughtful gift and is reputed to relieve sore throats and raspy coughs.

MAKES ⅓ CUP
⅓ cup pale, runny, preferably
organic, honey
5 cups scented rose petals

Put the honey and rose petals in an enamel pan and boil gently for ten minutes. Strain the honey while it is still quite hot and put into a warm, sterilized jar with a tight-fitting lid. When the jar is cold, label and date.

Rose-water Cookies

These light, crunchy cookies are easy to make and bake in minutes.

1 cup lightly salted butter
1 cup caster sugar
1 large egg
1 tbsp light cream
2½ cups all-purpose flour
½ tsp salt
1 tsp baking powder
1 tbsp rose water
sugar for sprinkling
Oven temperature: 375°F

Soften the butter and mix with all the other ingredients until you have a firm dough. Mould the mixture into an even roll and wrap in greaseproof paper. Chill until it is firm enough to slice very thinly. This may take between one and one and a half hours.

Line baking sheets with some nonstick parchment paper and arrange the cookies on the sheets with enough space for them to

Left: The rose here is 'Amber Queen', but you can add any scented rose petals to the honey.

spread. Sprinkle with a little sugar and bake for about ten minutes until they are just turning brown at the edges.

Festival Shortbreads

This Greek version of shortbread, one of the world's most popular sweet cookies, keeps well for a long time in the delicately flavored sugar, which may be used up in other recipes after the cookies have been eaten.

1 generous cup unsalted or
lightly salted butter
⅓ cup sugar
1 large egg yolk
2 tbsp Greek ouzo, Pernod or brandy
4 oz unblanched almonds
½ generous cup cornstarch
2¾ cups all-purpose flour
about 4 tbsp triple-distilled rose water
2¾ cups confectioners' sugar
Oven temperature:
325–350°F

Cream the butter and add the sugar, egg yolk and alcohol. Grind the almonds, skins and all: they should be much coarser and browner than commercially ground almonds. Add to the butter mixture and then work in the cornstarch and enough flour to give a firm, soft mixture (you may need a little more flour).

Above: The roses toward the back of the picture are the striped petalled rose, 'Henri Matisse', and the exotic-colored rose, 'Gray Dawn'.

You can mix it in an electric mixer or a food processor.

Divide into 24–28 portions. Make them into little rolls and then into crescents around your finger. Place on baking sheets lined with parchment paper and bake for 15 minutes. Check the biscuits and lower the temperature if they seem to be coloring. Bake for another five to ten minutes in any case. Let cool.

Pour the rose water into a small bowl and put the sifted confectioners' sugar into a larger one. Dip a biscuit into the rose water, sprinkle it with confectioners' sugar and place in an airtight tin. Repeat until all the biscuits are coated. Pack the biscuits loosely otherwise they will stick together. Sift the remaining icing sugar over the biscuits and keep them in the airtight container.

BALTI ROSE-MIX SPICES

Balti is a style of cooking that originated in Baltistan, now part of northern Pakistan, in an area enclosed by the world's highest mountain ranges – the Himalayas, the Karakorams and the Hindu Kush. Though this is one of the toughest places on earth, often cut off for months on end by snow and ice, people have lived there since 3000 BC.

The type of curry that has evolved from Baltistan is cooked in a *karahi* or Balti pan which is a cast-iron, wok-like dish with two handles. A large saucepan or wok may be substituted. Food is also eaten from the same dish. It is always freshly cooked using aromatic spices rather than the hot chilies popular in the south. Balti is traditionally served without rice or cutlery – pieces of bread or naan are used to scoop up the curry.

Dried rose petals are an ingredient in the Balti version of *garam masala*, a mixture of spices used extensively in cooking. Fresh rose petals are used to decorate many dishes and are added to fresh salads. A small bowl of rose-scented water decorated with rose petals may be presented at Balti meals for guests to wash their fingers. All over India and Pakistan, rose-water and oil or essence are added to the very sweet dishes served after meals, which are usually milk-based.

Balti Garam Masala

Garam masala means hot spices, but this Balti version has an emphasis on aromatic flavoring rather than a hot sensation. The mixture is added at the end of the cooking.

MAKES ABOUT 1¾ CUPS

2½ oz coriander seeds (dhania)
1½ oz white cumin seeds (jeera safed)
1 oz aniseed (soonf chotti)
1 oz cassia bark (dalchini)
1 oz green cardamom seeds (elaichi motti)
½ oz cloves (lavang)
20 dried mint leaves
12 bay leaves (tej patia)
30 dried scented rose petals (gulab patti)
5 saffron stamens (zafraan)

Rose petals are included in Balti Garam Masala.

Toast all the ingredients lightly under a low broiler or roast in a slow oven. The spices should give off a light steam, but be careful not to let them burn. When they start to give off an aroma, remove from the heat and cool. Grind well and mix together before storing them in an airtight jar. Keep in a cool dark cupboard. This mixture will keep for several months, but for the best flavor, make it fresh every month.

Balti Masala Paste

The base for most Balti dishes is this mild-flavored paste to which meat, fish and vegetables may be added and stir-fried. This paste would make an ideal present for a committed curry lover.

¾ cup Balti garam masala
¾ cup white wine vinegar
¾ cup light vegetable oil
(not olive oil)

Mix together the *garam masala* and vinegar in a bowl with enough water to make a thick, creamy paste. Let stand for about 30 minutes. Heat the oil in a heavy-bottomed saucepan and add the paste carefully. Stir-fry until all the water has evaporated and the liquid is reduced

Use only good-quality, authentic spices in making your own Balti garam masala.

– this should take about five to ten minutes. The mixture is cooked when the saucepan is taken off the heat and no oil is floating to the surface after about three minutes.

Bottle the paste in warm, sterilized jars capped with a little hot oil. Seal the jars well, labeling and dating when they are cold. Keep in a cool dark cupboard, but refrigerate after a jar is opened.

An Authentic Balti Meal

Balti Salad

A lightly spiced salad is a welcome accompaniment to rich food.

SERVES 4

2 tbsp sesame oil

1 tsp black mustard seeds

1 garlic clove, finely chopped

1 tsp grated fresh ginger

1 tsp rose-flavored vinegar (optional)

2/3 cup white cabbage leaves, finely shredded

1 cup baby spinach leaves

1½ cups celeriac, finely grated

1 medium carrot, shredded

1 zucchini, julienned

10 snow peas, roughly chopped

1 cup fresh bean sprouts

freshly squeezed lemon juice

salt and pepper

4 cups freshly prepared scented rose petals

Heat the oil and stir-fry the mustard seeds for about ten seconds. Add the garlic and continue frying for 30 seconds. Remove from the heat. When the oil is cold, mix with the ginger and rose-flavored vinegar and then add to the prepared vegetables. Season to taste and keep cool before serving with a good sprinkling of lemon juice and adding the rose petals as an edible decoration.

Balti Chicken Curry

To give the sauce a rich red color, you can use 2 tsp beet powder and anatto seed powder. Alternatively, a few drops of red and sunset yellow food coloring will produce the same result but don't overdo the quantity or the dish will look very artificial.

Balti Salad decorated with fresh rose petals.

SERVES 4

3 tbsp ghee or corn oil

4 cloves of garlic, finely chopped

1¼ cups onion, peeled and coarsely chopped

4 tbsp Balti masala paste

8 tomatoes, quartered

2 green bell peppers, seeds removed and roughly chopped

4 cups skinned and boned chicken, cut into bite-sized cubes

1 scant cup chicken stock or water

1 tbsp Balti garam masala

1 tbsp fresh cilantro leaves, finely chopped (optional)

Heat the ghee or oil in a *karahi*, wok or large saucepan until very hot and sauté the garlic for 20 seconds. Add the onion, reduce heat and fry (about ten minutes) until the onion becomes translucent. Add the *masala* paste, tomatoes, peppers and chicken and increase the heat enough to stir-fry for about five minutes. Add the stock or water and simmer for about 20 minutes, stirring every two to three minutes.

Test to see if the chicken is cooked before adding the *garam masala* and cilantro leaves. Season and serve with Balti salad and Naan.

A traditional Balti meal of Balti Chicken Curry, Balti Salad and Naan bread.

Balti Naan

Originally these breads were brought to Baltistan by the Ancient Persians and were cooked on the sides of the *tandoor* or clay oven. The traditional tear shape occurs because the dough is pressed on the neck of the *tandoor* and gravity naturally elongates the bread. If you are using a more conventional grill, you can mold the bread to this shape or, if desired, make it square or triangular.

MAKES 8–10

4 cups strong white bread flour

1 tbsp baking powder

1 tbsp sugar

2 tbsp strained Greek yogurt

1 tsp salt

2 tsp toasted sesame seeds

½ tsp mustard seeds

a little ghee or melted butter

Make a dough by working together all the ingredients except the ghee or butter with your fingers, using a little warm water. Knead on a floured board, place in a bowl and leave in a warm place for two to three hours to prove. Knead again and divide into balls. Roll each ball on a floured surface into a disk about 10 inches in diameter and ¼ inch thick.

Preheat the broiler and cover the rack with foil. Put the bread under the broiler and watch it carefully. When brown patches appear, turn the bread, brushing the uncooked side with a little ghee or butter. Return to the broiler until the bread is sizzling. Serve immediately.

ROSE ICES

Rose Ice Cream

A very rich, creamy ice cream lightly flavored
with lemon and rose.

6 large egg yolks

7 tbsp sugar

1¼ cups milk

1¼ cups light cream

*½ tsp finely grated lemon peel (preferably from
an unwaxed lemon)*

1 tbsp triple-distilled rose water

⅔ cup heavy cream

candied rose petals for decoration

Beat the egg yolks and sugar together for five
to ten minutes until the sugar has dissolved.
Heat the milk and light cream in a double-
boiler but do not boil. Pour the liquid into the
egg yolk mixture, gently beating all the time.
Replace in the double-boiler together with the
lemon peel and rose water. Heat over very hot
water until the mixture becomes sticky.

Let the mixture cool and then whisk in the
heavy cream. Freeze in an ice-cream maker or
a freezer tray. If using a freezer tray, remove the
ice cream after an hour, blend in a food
processor and freeze again. Repeat this step,
and the ice cream will set in three hours.

Syllabub

This pudding dates back centuries and is light
in texture with just enough lemon to avoid it
being too rich.

SERVES 4–6

2 lemons (preferably unwaxed)

1 glass dry white or dessert wine or pale sherry

3 tbsp sugar

1 pint heavy cream

4 tsp triple-distilled rose water

a few candied rose petals

Grate the lemon peel finely and marinate it
with the wine or sherry, the juice of one lemon
and the sugar. Let sit for at least six hours.

Combine the mixture with the cream, the
juice from the remaining lemon and the rose
water in a large bowl and whip until it stands
up in soft peaks. Serve chilled in glasses and
decorate with candied rose petals.

Rose and Pear Sorbet

A light, fruity alternative to the calorie-laden
desserts found in restaurants.

SERVES 2–4

2 William or Comice pears

1¼ cups water

2 tbsp sugar

*½ cup Sauternes, or other
sweet white wine*

1 egg white

1 tbsp rose water

fresh rose petals or candied rose heads

Peel, quarter and core the pears and poach
them gently in the water and sugar for about
20 minutes. Drain the pears and blend them in
a food processor with the wine. Freeze the
mixture until it is the consistency of soft snow.

Whisk the egg white until stiff and
gradually add it to the fruit and wine mixture.
Fold in the rose water and refreeze the sorbet
for four hours. Remove from the freezer about
20 minutes before serving. Decorate with fresh
rose petals or candied rose heads.

From left to right: Rose Sorbet, Syllabub and Ice Cream.

ROSE CHEESECAKE AND PASHKA

As well as having rose flavors in your desserts, it is also a lovely idea to decorate your dishes with candied rose petals. They make a winning touch to any display.

Rose and Raspberry Cheesecake

7 oz pie-crust pastry

egg yolk for brushing pastry

¾ cup fermented cheese or low fat cream cheese

3 tbsp plain Greek yogurt

1 tsp finely grated lemon zest (preferably from an unwaxed lemon)

2 tsp triple-distilled rose water

1 tbsp sugar

3 cups raspberries (or any combination of soft fruits)

2 tbsp Rose Jelly (or red currant jelly)

Oven temperature: 400°F

This light summer tart could be made with a combination of fruits such as strawberries, and red currants.

1 *Line a well-buttered, fluted 8 in flan ring with the pastry and prick with a fork. Cover the pastry base with waxed paper and fill with baking beans or dried chick-peas. Brush the edges with egg yolk and bake for 15 minutes. Remove the paper and beans, cook for a further ten minutes, until the pastry is golden. Allow to cool.*

2 *Cream the soft cheese and blend with the yogurt, lemon rind, rose water and sugar. Fill the cooled pastry case and spread smoothly. Arrange the raspberries around the edge of the cheesecake. Heat the jelly until runny and brush over the raspberries. For special occasions, decorate with candied rose petals or whole blooms.*

Rose Pashka

In Russia a version of this creamy dessert is traditionally served at Easter made in a special wooden mold, but a simple clay flowerpot, washed and scrubbed well and baked in a hot oven for 30 minutes, will do just as well.

4 tbsp light cream
2 large yolks
⅓ cup sugar
scant ½ cup unsalted butter
1½ cups cottage cheese
1½ cups mascarpone cheese
2 tsp triple-distilled rose water
½ cup chopped candied orange peel
½ cup chopped blanched almonds
candied roses as decoration

The rose decorations add elegance to this dish.

1 *Heat the cream to just below boiling point. Beat the egg yolks with the sugar until light and foamy and add to the cream. Heat together in a saucepan until the mixture thickens, taking care not to let it boil and curdle. Remove from the heat and cool. Beat the butter until creamy and add to the egg and cream mixture, adding the cheeses slowly then the rose water, candied peel and nuts.*

2 *Line the flowerpot with cheesecloth and spoon the mixture into it, covering the top with cheese-cloth. Weight a small plate on the top of the flowerpot and stand it on a plate in the refrigerator for about six hours or overnight. Turn out the pashka by inverting the flowerpot onto a serving dish and remove the cheesecloth. Decorate the bottom of the dish with the candied roses.*

ROSE PETAL PAVLOVA

If you are making ice cream, a delicious way to use up the egg whites is to make a Pavlova: then you have not just one but two delicious puddings to serve your guests!

SERVES 4–6

4 large egg whites

¾ cup sugar

4 tbsp Rose Jelly (or red currant jelly)

1¼ cups heavy cream or

ricotta cheese

2¾ cups mixed soft fruits

fresh and candied rose petals

for decoration

Oven temperature: 275°F

Cut out an 8 inch waxed paper circle and place on a baking tray. Whisk the egg whites until stiff and slowly whisk in the sugar until the mixture makes stiff, glossy peaks. Spoon the meringue onto the paper circle, making a slight indentation in the center and soft crests around the outside. Bake for one to one and a half hours until the meringue is crisp. Take care not to let it turn brown. Turn off the oven and let the meringue cool in the oven.

Immediately before serving, melt the jelly over a low heat and spread in the center. Spoon over the cream or ricotta cheese and arrange the soft fruits and rose petals on top. The dish should be eaten straight away.

Left: Add candied petals among the fruit as an added decoration.

Right: Why not make the Pavlova the table center-piece by surrounding it with fresh greenery from the garden?

SOURCES AND SUPPLIERS

U.K.

ROSE SOCIETIES

The Royal National Rose
  Society
(membership includes free publi-
  cations, advice, shows and
  garden visits)
contact The Secretary
The Royal National Rose
  Society
Chiswell Green
St Albans
Herts AL2 3NR
Tel: 01727 850461

British Rose Growers
  Association
303 Mile End Road
Colchester
Essex
CO4 5EA

ROSE GROWERS
(including Old Roses, personal
  shoppers and by mail order)

David Austin Roses
Bowling Green Lane
Albrighton
Wolverhampton WV7 3HB
Tel: 01902 373931

Le Grice Roses
Norwich Road
North Walsham
Norfolk NR28 0DR
Tel: 01692 402591

Peter Beales Roses
London Road
Attleborough
Norfolk NR17 1AY
Tel: 01953 454707

Cottage Garden Roses
Woodlands House
Stretton
near Stafford ST19 9LG
Tel: 01785 840217

ESSENTIAL OIL SUPPLIERS
(shops and mail order)

G Baldwin & Co
173 Walworth Road
London SE17 1RW

Tel: 0171 703 5550

Neal's Yard Remedies
5 Golden Cross
Cornmarket Street
Oxford OX1 3EU
Tel: 01865 245436

Culpeper Ltd
Hadstock Road
Linton
Cambridge
CB1 6NJ
Tel: 01440 788196

Maurene Charlwood
(aromatherapist)
13 Weald Close
Shalford
Surrey

DRIED ROSES
(personal shoppers and mail
  order)

The Hop Shop
Castle Farm
Shoreham
Sevenoaks
Kent TN14 7UB
Tel: 01959 523219

GLOVES AND PRUNING
  EQUIPMENT

Burton McCall Ltd
163 Parker Drive
Leicester LE4 0JP
Tel: 0116 234 0800

U.S.A.

ROSE SOCIETIES

American Rose Society
Box 300000
Shreveport, LA 711390
Tel: (318) 938-5402

Heritage Roses Foundation
Mr Charles A. Walker Jr.
1512 Gorman Street
Raleigh, NC 27606

American Horticultural Society
7931 East Boulevard Drive
Alexandria, VA 22308
Tel: (703) 768-5700

ROSE GROWERS
(including mail order suppliers)

Armstrong Roses
P. O. Box 4220
Huntington Station, NY 11746
Tel: (800) 321-6640

Lowe's Own-root Roses
6 Sheffield Road
Nashua, NH 03062
Tel: (603) 888-2214

Jackson and Perkins
1 Rose Lane
Medford, OR 97501
Tel: (800) USA-ROSE

NATURAL BEAUTY
  INGREDIENTS

The Body Shop
45 Horse Hill Road
Cedar Knolls, NY 07927-2014
Tel: (800) 541-2535

Kiehl's
109 Third Avenue
New York, NY 10002
Tel: (212) 677-3171

Lorann Oils
P. O. Box 22009
Lansing, MI 48909-2009
Tel: (800) 248-1302

GLOVES AND PRUNING
  EQUIPMENT

Smith and Hawken
P. O. Box 6900
Florence, KY 41022 6900
Tel: (800) 776-5558

Gardener's Eden
P. O. Box 7307
San Francisco, CA 94120 7307
Tel: (800) 822-1214

SUPPLIERS OF DRIED FLOWERS
(shops and mail order)

Dody Lyness Co.
7336 Berry Hill Drive
Palos Verdes Peninsula, CA
  90274
Tel: (310) 377-7040

Gailann's Floral Catalog
821 W. Atlantic Street
Branson, MO 65616

Nature's Finest
P. O. Box 10311, Dept. CSS
Burke, VA 22009

Val's Naturals
P. O. Box 832
Kathleen, FL 33849
Tel: (813) 858-8991

AUSTRALIA

ROSE SOCIETIES

National Rose Society
271B Belmore Road
North Balwyn, Vic 3104
Tel: (03) 9857 9656

Rose Society in Victoria
P. O. Box 1004
Blackburn North Vic 3130
Tel: (03) 9877 4301

Rose Society of NSW
299 Malton Road
North Epping NSW 2121
Tel: (02) 869 7516

Queensland Rose Society Inc
GPO Box 1866
Brisbane Qld 4001
Tel: (07) 814 4714

Rose Society of South Australia
29 Columbia Crescent
Modbury North SA 5092
Tel: (002) 663 366

Rose Society of Tasmania
RSD 146 Cradoc Hill Road
Cradoc Hill Tas 7109
Tel: (002) 458 6452

Rose Society of W.A.
33 Lord St
Bentley WA 6102
Tel: (09) 458 6452

ROSE GROWERS AND
  NURSERIES

The Perfumed Garden
895 Derril Road
Moorooduc
Victoria 3933

Swane's Nursery
490 Galston Road
Dural
NSW, 2158
Tel: (02) 651 1322

Doyles Rose Farm
1389 Waterford Tambourine
  Road
Logan Village
QLD 4207
Tel: (07) 5546 8216

Brundrett & Sons (Roses) Pty
  Ltd
Brundrett Road
Narre Warren North
Victoria, 3804
Tel: (03) 9596 8742

SUPPLIERS

Hedgerow Flowers
177 King William Road
Hyde Park
SA 5061
Tel: (08) 373 4779

Roses Only
Shop 12, Chifley Plaza
Chifley Square
Sydney NSW 2000
Tel: (02) 232 4499

The Gardener's Book Service
211 Bay Street
Brighton
Victoria 3186
Tel: (03) 9596 8742

INDEX

AUTHOR'S ACKNOWLEDGMENTS

I have always loved roses and it has been a real pleasure to research and write a book about them. Thank you, Joanna Lorenz, for that. I would like to thank rose growers and breeders everywhere but in particular, Peter Beales, his assistant Simon White and Bill Le Grice for giving me some of their most beautiful roses and sharing their expertise. Many thanks to David Austin for letting Lucy Mason photograph his rose gardens. Thank you Patzi for making the mouthwatering rose recipes and for expertly candying scores of rose-heads and petals. Many thanks to Gilli Hanna for creating the gorgeous rose bags and sachets, and to Chris Jones for designing and making the prize-winning buttonholes and corsages. To Maurene Charlwood for her beauty formulas, to Kent Turnefelt for his Swedish Sweets and to Lisa Tai for designing these pages. And my special thanks to Michelle Garrett and her assistant Dulcie who gently and creatively transformed my ideas into glorious pictures and finally to Helen Sudell who managed this project with immense skill.

PICTURE ACKNOWLEDGEMENTS

AKG: p13 (left), p15. **ET Archive:** p11, p12, p14. **David Austin Roses:** p28 (left), p29. **Clive Nicholls:** p20 (both), p27 (top and right), p30 (both), p31 (both), p36. **Visual Arts Library:** p10, p13 (right).